SOMETHING
FOR THE WEEKEND

SOMETHING FOR THE WEEKEND

Simon Rimmer & Tim Lovejoy

Quadrille
PUBLISHING

Photography by William Reavell

This edition first published in 2010 by Quadrille
Publishing Limited
Alhambra House, 27–31 Charing Cross Road,
London WC2H 0LS

This book was previously published in 2008 as
Lazy Brunch

Editorial Director Jane O'Shea
Creative Director Helen Lewis
Project Editor Laura Herring
Designer Katherine Case
Photographer William Reavell
Photographer's Assistant Megan Brady
Food Stylist Valerie Berry
Assistant Food Stylist Georgina Foottit
Production Vincent Smith, Bridget Fish

Text © 2008 Simon Rimmer, Tim Lovejoy
and Princess Productions
Photography © 2008 William Reavell
Design and layout © 2008 Quadrille Publishing Limited

Cataloguing in Publication Data:
a catalogue record for this book is available from
the British Library.

ISBN 978 184400 907 7

Printed in China

PRINCESS PRODUCTIONS

Princess Productions
Managing Directors Henrietta
Conrad and Sebastian Scott
Series Producer Catherine Mann
Food Producer JoJo Strous
Home Economists Claire
Bassano and Yasmin Othman

Princess Productions
Unit 316 Whiteleys Centre
151 Queensway
London W2 4YN

contents

introduction 6

1. beers with the boys 10

2. treating your girlfriend 36

3. food to share 62

4. the olds round for brunch 88

5. dishes to impress 114

index 140

acknowledgements 144

introduction

From Simon:

I knew that Tim and I were going to get on as soon as we met. He told me he didn't cook, didn't really like cookery programmes and had no real interest in them…add on to that the fact that he supports Chelsea F.C. and you can see it was a match made in heaven.

The thing is, though, is that Tim likes a challenge, is very competitive and hates not being good at something, and so, little by little, he began to enjoy the cooking on the show. He wanted to learn how to chop, why flavours worked well together, what happened if you added more chilli etc. And basically that's what this book is all about. If you're an enthusiastic novice, like Lovejoy, all the recipes are simple, straightforward and tasty – no fancy techniques, just good, honest food. And if, like me, you can do a bit of cooking already, you'll find some new recipe ideas to dazzle your diners.

We've split the book into five sections with different themes – Beers with the Boys, Treating your Girlfriend, Food to Share, The Olds Round for Brunch and Dishes to Impress…so you can pick your favourites from each chapter and just go for it, or feel free to mix and match. If you're likely to impress your girlfriend with a salmon burger or eat sushi with the boys over several beers, then happy days.

You'll also learn some secrets that you'd never thought you'd know. The mystery of the scotch egg: do you, like Tim, think you have to carve a hole out of the sausage meat and squeeze the egg inside? The pork pie: how come the pastry's so crunchy and the pork so, well, 'porky'? And chicken Kievs: how come the garlic butter doesn't ooze out while they're cooking? So, you can cook 'em all and then either pass on the secrets or keep them safe with smug satisfaction. Knowledge is power.

One of the best things about *Something for the Weekend* is how much feedback I get on the recipes – how many of you lie in bed watching us with a big fat hangover! It seems *Something for the Weekend* is what you all need – simple food, something to fill you up, make you feel good and make you want to get into the kitchen and start cooking. So get your pinny on, make the food and live the dream…but just one thing: don't be like Tim and call me on Boxing Day morning to ask me how to cook a capon.

From Tim:

When a friend of yours is a top notch chef like Simon, as if you're NOT going to phone him up for cooking advice! But, now that Simon has helped me to develop my own cooking skills, I'm beginning to feel more confident in the kitchen. I particularly enjoy chopping – I've learnt that I need to stand like a gun slinger and tuck my fingers under my knuckles. I practise my technique on onions and peppers and I'm getting pretty good.

I've also learnt weird facts about food: vanilla pods come from orchids and who would have thought that cinnamon is actually bark? I now know that you should never eat neat saffron and that I dislike goat's milk as much as goat's cheese.

But I have to admit that my favourite part of doing *Something for the Weekend* is getting to eat all of Simon's brilliant dishes. Everything he cooks tastes fantastic, but favourites of mine, so far, are the chicken Kiev, the scotch eggs and the smoked salmon hash. Bring it on!

When I was asked to do *Something for the Weekend* I never imagined that I'd become so interested in cooking, but Simon's the man!

An extra note from Simon:

Before you start cooking, be sure to read the recipe through to the end and check that you have all the required equipment and ingredients. We do use a food processor quite lot, so it may be a good idea to invest in one. And if you want to make the pork pie, it'd be a good idea to get yourself a pork pie tin or a muffin tray (which is great for making smaller pork pies in).

Also, be aware that some of the recipes require additional chilling, resting or marinating time – and a few need a little pre-preparation a day or two in advance – so check your timings carefully.

1

beers
with the
boys

big sausage rolls

scotch eggs

pots of noodles

corned beef fritters

beef empanadas

shrimp po'boys

cheese and
potato pasties

crispy fried chicken

cheesy potato pies

veggie chilli tacos

smoked haddock tempura

salmon burgers

scotch eggs

The biggest EVER success on the show. Tim called me one morning to ask how you made them. 'Do you make the outside, then put the egg in the middle?'…I so wanted to say 'yes'.

Serves 4

5 free-range eggs
275g sausage meat
1 tsp fresh thyme leaves
1 tbsp chopped fresh parsley
1 spring onion, very finely chopped
salt and freshly ground black pepper
125g plain flour, well seasoned
85g breadcrumbs
400ml vegetable oil

Serve the scotch eggs with crisps, lager and pickled onions.

1 Place 4 eggs, in their shells, in a pan of cold salted water. Over a high heat, bring to the boil, then simmer for 9 minutes. Cool under cold running water, then peel.

2 In a bowl, mix the sausage meat with the thyme, parsley and spring onion. Season generously, especially with black pepper.

3 Divide the mixture into four and, using your hands, flatten each portion into an oval measuring 13cm x 7.5cm at its widest points.

4 Place the seasoned flour in a shallow bowl and dredge each boiled egg in it.

5 Place a floured egg on each of the sausage-meat ovals and wrap the sausage meat around the egg, making sure that the coating is smooth and it completely covers each egg.

6 Beat the remaining egg in a shallow bowl. Roll a sausage meat-coated egg in the beaten egg and then in the breadcrumbs to cover completely. Repeat with the other eggs. Preheat the oven to 180°C/350°F/gas mark 4.

7 Pour the vegetable oil into a deep, heavy-bottomed saucepan, ensuring that it is no more than two-thirds full. Heat over a medium flame. When you can drop a breadcrumb into the oil and it sizzles and turns brown, it is hot enough to cook the scotch eggs. (It will be about 180°C/350°F, which you can check using a kitchen thermometer. Needless to say, be very careful with the hot oil and never leave it unattended.)

8 Place the scotch eggs in the hot oil. Cook for about 8 minutes, until golden and crisp and the sausage meat is cooked through. Carefully remove the eggs with a slotted spoon and drain on some kitchen paper.

9 To ensure they are properly cooked pop them in the oven for a further 7–8 minutes. Remove and leave to cool.

top tip:

To stop the sausage meat sticking to your fingers as you wrap it round the egg, lay the sausage meat oval on cling film and place the egg on top. Use the cling film to bring the sausage around the egg and mould into a ball shape.

big sausage rolls

These are so easy to make, but equally easy to be disappointing. What you need to remember when making any kind of 'sausagey' food is that seasoning is king. However much salt and pepper you think you need, add a bit more to get the taste just right.

Serves 4

30g butter
100g button mushrooms, finely chopped
1 tbsp Worcestershire sauce
1 tbsp Tabasco sauce
1 tbsp dried thyme
375g sausage meat
salt and freshly ground black pepper
375g ready-rolled puff pastry
1 free-range egg, beaten

Serve the sausage rolls with ketchup or pickle.

1 Preheat the oven to 200°C/400°F/gas mark 6.

2 Melt the butter in a large frying pan and fry the mushrooms until soft. Allow to cool.

3 Transfer the mushrooms to a large bowl and add the Worcestershire sauce, Tabasco sauce, thyme and sausage meat. Season well with salt and pepper and mix thoroughly to combine.

4 Cut the pastry into four equal-sized rectangles.

5 Lay some of the sausage meat mixture down the centre of each pastry strip and brush one edge of the pastry with the beaten egg. Fold the other side of the pastry over and press to seal. Trim off any excess pastry.

6 Place the sausage rolls on a baking tray and cook in the oven for 18–20 minutes, until the pastry is crisp and golden and the sausage meat has cooked through.

top tip:

To get really super-shiny pastry, glaze the sausage roll once, put it in the fridge for 20 minutes and then glaze it again before you cook it.

pots of noodles

See what we've done? Noodles are one of the best fast foods: tasty, easy to make and you can be very inventive with the ingredients…a bit like here.

Serves 4

4 asparagus spears, sliced
4 sheets egg noodles
  (about 230g)
100ml light soy sauce
100ml vegetable stock
juice of 2 limes
1 garlic clove, crushed
25mm ginger, cut into
  matchsticks
1 tbsp cornflour, mixed with a
  little water to create a paste
1 tbsp vegetable oil
1 red onion, finely sliced
200g shiitake mushrooms,
  finely sliced
1 red pepper, diced
1 small red chilli, chopped
1 tbsp coriander, chopped

Serve the noodles in bowls, pour over the sauce and garnish with a little fresh coriander.

1 Drop the asparagus spears into a pan of boiling water. Cook for a minute then remove the spears from the hot water with a slotted spoon. Transfer the asparagus to a bowl of ice-cold water. This will retain their texture and colour.

2 Cook the egg noodles according to the packet instructions.

3 Place the soy sauce, vegetable stock, lime juice, garlic and ginger in a small pan over a medium heat. Bring to the boil and cook for 5 minutes.

4 Add the cornflour paste and stir well to thicken the sauce.

5 Meanwhile, heat the oil in a pan over a high heat. Stir-fry the onion, mushrooms, red pepper, chilli, coriander and asparagus for 5–6 minutes, until just softened.

6 Add the noodles and mix together well.

top tip:

If you use cornflour to thicken sauces, always use your finger to mix it, so you can feel when all the lumps have gone.

corned beef fritters

Beer and fried food is a match made in heaven. The much maligned tin of corned beef is the star performer here. Think of 'beefy' as that squad player coming off the bench to score the winner in your local derby, you never knew he had it in him…well he does.

Serves 4

For the corned beef fritters
400g can corned beef,
  cut into 2.5cm thick pieces
125g plain flour
½ tsp turmeric
1 tsp salt
1 free-range egg
1 free-range egg yolk
140ml whole milk
1 tbsp olive oil
1 free-range egg white
400ml vegetable oil
4 free-range eggs

For the onion marmalade
50ml olive oil
2 large onions, chopped
2 red bird's eye chillies, chopped
4 cloves
1 garlic clove, crushed
juice and zest of 1 orange
150ml sherry vinegar
150g soft light brown sugar
salt and freshly ground black
  pepper

top tip:
Beat the batter with a fork, not a whisk, so that you don't break down the gluten in the flour too much.

Serve the fritters topped with the poached eggs and a little of the onion marmalade.

The corned beef fritters

1 Sift the flour, turmeric and salt into a bowl. Make a well in the centre of the flour mixture. Add the whole egg and the egg yolk and whisk together to create a paste. Gently fold the milk and olive oil into the egg paste to form a batter. Whisk the egg white until soft peaks form and then fold into the batter. Dip the corned beef pieces into the batter mixture.

2 Pour the vegetable oil into a deep, heavy-bottomed saucepan, ensuring that it is no more than two-thirds full. Heat over a medium flame. When you can drop a breadcrumb into the oil and it sizzles and turns brown, it is hot enough to cook the corned beef. (The oil will be about 180°C/350°F. Needless to say, be very careful with the hot oil and never leave it unattended.)

3 Fry the corned beef in the hot oil for about 6 minutes, until crisp and golden-brown. Carefully remove and drain on kitchen paper.

4 Heat a pan of water over a medium heat. Reduce the heat to low and gently break two eggs into the water. Cook for 5 minutes, or until the whites are firm. Remove with a slotted spoon, set aside and cover to keep warm while you poach the other eggs.

The onion marmalade
Heat the oil in a frying pan over a medium heat and gently fry the onion, chilli, cloves and garlic for about 15 minutes, until soft and caramelised. Add the orange juice and zest, sherry vinegar and sugar and bring to the boil. Cook out for about 10–20 minutes, until the mixture is the consistency of jam. Season, to taste, with salt and pepper.

beef empanadas

If you think that some of the Mexican food we eat in the UK is a bit bland and lacks that South American flair, then these fellas will restore your faith. Bite-sized, tasty, firey and addictive – bring it on.

Makes 12

For the pastry
225g plain flour, plus extra
  for dusting
½ tsp turmeric
½ tsp chilli flakes
75g chilled butter, cut into cubes
pinch of salt
50–75ml milk
1 free-range egg yolk
1 free-range egg, beaten

For the filling
1 tbsp olive oil
1 onion, finely chopped
1 garlic clove, crushed
1 carrot, finely diced
225g extra lean ground beef
1 tbsp tomato purée
¾ tsp ground cumin
1 tsp chilli powder
1 potato, peeled, cut into
  small cubes
100ml dark Mexican beer (*negro modelo*), brown ale or stout

top tip:
Be careful with flavoured pastry as it can dry out quickly. Reduce the quantity of flour to counteract this.

Serve the empanadas on a large plate with a bowl of sweet chilli sauce or smoked habanero sauce.

The pastry
1 Place the flour, turmeric, chilli flakes, butter and salt in a food processor and pulse until the mixture has the consistency of breadcrumbs. Add the milk and egg yolk and pulse until it forms a dough. (Add 50ml milk to begin with and more if it seems too dry.)

2 Turn the dough out onto a lightly floured surface and knead for a few minutes. Wrap in cling film and chill in the fridge for an hour.

The filling
1 Heat the oil in a frying pan over a medium heat and fry the onions, garlic and carrot until soft.

2 Add the mince and fry for 3–4 minutes, until the meat has browned lightly all over. Stir in the tomato purée, cumin and chilli powder and cook for 3–4 minutes.

3 Add the cubed potatoes and beer and bring to the boil. Reduce the heat and simmer for 25 minutes, or until potatoes are cooked. Leave to cool.

To assemble the empanadas
1 Preheat the oven to 200°C/400°F/gas mark 6. Remove the pastry from the fridge and roll it out onto a floured surface, until it has the thickness of a pound coin. Using a knife cut out twelve circles, about 12cm in diameter.

2 Place a spoonful of the filling in the middle of each pastry circle. Brush the edge of one half of each circle with beaten egg. Fold over and press to seal – make sure you don't trap any air inside the pastry parcel. Mark the edges using the tines of a fork.

3 Place on a baking tray and cook in the oven for 10–15 minutes, until the pastry is golden and the filling is hot.

shrimp po' boys

I always know when Tim really likes a recipe, he tastes it and says 'Yeah, that's good…oh, that's really good, yeah that's great – I like that'. This was such a recipe. Word of warning, you need a big gob to do these justice.

Serves 4

200g polenta
200g plain flour
30g creole seasoning
  (see recipe below)
1 free-range egg
200ml milk
450g king prawns
200g brown shrimps
salt and freshly ground black
  pepper
4–5 tbsp vegetable oil
8 small soft torpedo rolls
  or 4 large rolls
8 Little Gem lettuce leaves
6 mini gherkins (cornichons),
  sliced lengthways
2 beef tomatoes, sliced
3 tbsp wholegrain mustard
Jamaican Hot Pepper Sauce
juice of 1 lemon

Serve these with extra pepper sauce for a bigger kick.

1 In a bowl, mix the polenta and flour with the creole seasoning.

2 In another bowl beat the egg and milk together.

3 Season the prawns and shrimps with salt and pepper. Dip them into the egg-and-milk mixture, then into the flour-and-polenta mixture, to coat.

4 Heat the oil in a frying pan over a medium heat and fry the prawns and shrimps for 4–6 minutes, turning once or twice, until they are crisp and golden brown.

5 Cut the buns in half and fill with lettuce leaves, the sliced gherkins, tomatoes and some mustard. Top with the prawns and shrimps, a little hot sauce and sprinkle over the lemon juice.

Creole seasoning

You can buy this in good supermarkets or make a large batch by mixing 2 tablespoons each of onion powder, garlic powder, dried oregano, dried basil and hot paprika with 1 tablespoon each of dried thyme, black pepper, white pepper and celery salt.

top tip:

In order to ensure the prawns are fully coated in the creole seasoning, dip the prawns in flour first.

cheese
and potato
pasties
with walnut pastry

You know, a pasty isn't just something to eat after you've stopped at a motorway service station and that ends up leaving a pile of greasy crumbs all over your clothes. Make these delicious cheese and walnut beauties and discover the art of pasty making.

Serves 4

For the pasties
450g plain flour
200g butter
2 free-range eggs
salt and freshly ground black
  pepper
2–3 tbsp milk (if necessary)
150g crushed walnuts
200g new potatoes
1 red onion, cut into wedges
1–2 tbsp olive oil
salt and freshly ground black
  pepper
200g smoked Lancashire cheese
  (or any hard cheese), cubed
handful baby spinach leaves
1 free-range egg, beaten

For the chutney
2 tbsp vegetable oil
1 onion, sliced
1 garlic clove, finely sliced
1 chilli, finely chopped
25mm piece fresh ginger,
  sliced into matchsticks
450g carrots, peeled, grated
splash of green ginger wine
  or medium sherry
150g Demerara sugar
150ml white wine vinegar
¼ tsp ground cloves
1 tsp cinnamon

Serve the pasties while they are still warm with a handful of watercress and a large dollop of the chutney.

The pasties
1 In a food processor, pulse together the flour, butter, eggs, salt and pepper, milk and walnuts. Roll the mixture into a ball, cover with cling film and chill in the fridge for 2 hours. About an hour into the chilling time, preheat the oven to 180°C/350°F/gas mark 4.

2 Cook the potatoes in a large pan of boiling salted water, until tender. Allow to cool.

3 Spread the onion wedges out on a baking tray and drizzle with the olive oil. Mix together to coat the onions, season with salt and pepper, and roast in the oven for 30 minutes. Turn and baste the onions half way through cooking. Leave to cool slightly.

4 Using a rolling pin, roll the chilled pastry out until it is about 2.5mm thick. Place a small side plate or saucer (about 15cm in diameter) onto the pastry and cut around it with a knife. Repeat with the remaining pastry to make four circles. Preheat the oven to 200°C/400°F/gas mark 6.

5 Cut the potatoes into small cubes and combine with the cheese, spinach and red onions in a bowl. Season with salt and pepper and mix gently.

6 Place a spoonful of the potato mixture onto one half of each pastry circle, fold the pastry over, crimp the edge to seal and brush with the beaten egg, to glaze.

7 Place on a baking tray and bake in the oven for 20 minutes until crisp and golden – like a Cornish pasty. Cool slightly.

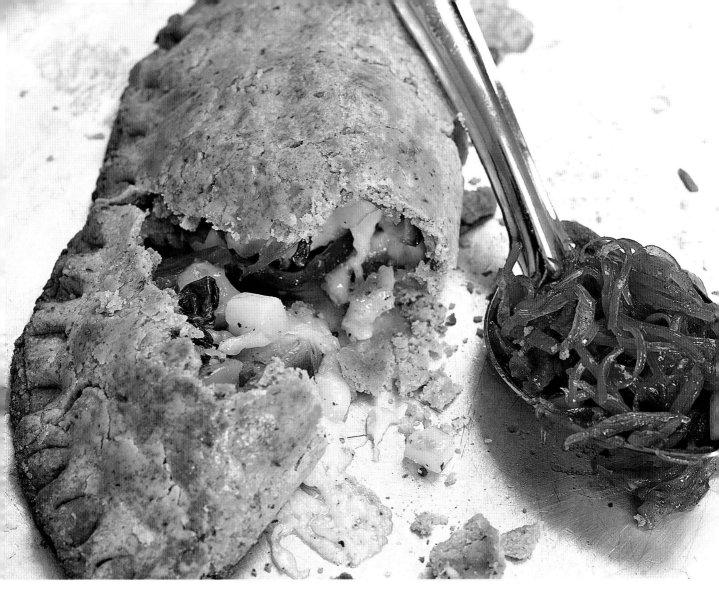

top tip:

If you plunge the walnuts in cold water first it will stop them tasting bitter.

The chutney

1 Heat the vegetable oil in a pan and fry the onion, garlic, chilli and ginger over a medium heat, until soft.

2 Add the carrot and cook for 10 minutes more.

3 Add the booze and simmer until nearly all the liquid has evaporated and it has reduced to almost nothing.

4 Add the sugar, vinegar and spices. Simmer for 15–25 minutes, until the mixture has a thick, jammy consistency. Leave to cool a little before serving.

crispy **fried chicken**
with guacamole

In the States and the Caribbean recipes and methods for fried chicken are taken very seriously, with many a family secret handed down from generation to generation. This one is a mix of all the best recipes I've stolen on my travels.

Serves 4

For the chicken
100ml tequila
juice of 3 limes
1 red chilli, chopped
330ml bottle Mexican beer
1 garlic clove, chopped
4 chicken legs or drumsticks
400ml vegetable oil
4 tbsp plain flour, well seasoned
   with 1 tsp chilli powder and
   salt and pepper

For the guacamole
2 ripe avocados, chopped
2 plum tomatoes, peeled,
   deseeded, chopped
1 bird's eye chilli, chopped
1 tbsp coriander stems
½ tsp chilli powder
juice 1 lime

For the pico de gallo
1 red onion, finely chopped
1 red chilli, finely chopped
juice 2 limes
2 tomatoes, chopped

top tip:
If the avocados are not ripe enough, microwave them for 15 seconds, and then they should be easier to peel.

Serve the chicken pieces with bowls of the guacamole and the pico de gallo.

The chicken
1 Mix the tequila, lime juice, chilli, beer and garlic together in a large bowl.

2 Using a sharp knife, score the chicken legs, then place them in the marinade. Mix well to coat the chicken and leave in the fridge for 2 hours to marinate.

3 Pour the vegetable oil into a deep, heavy-bottomed saucepan, ensuring that it is no more than two-thirds full. Heat over a medium flame. When you can drop a breadcrumb into the oil and it sizzles and turns brown, it is hot enough to cook the chicken. (It will be about 180°C/350°F, which you can check using a kitchen thermometer. Needless to say, be very careful with the hot oil and never leave it unattended.)

4 Meanwhile, remove the chicken from the marinade and roll it through the seasoned flour.

5 Place the chicken in the hot oil. Deep fry for 15–20 minutes, until golden brown and cooked through. Drain on kitchen paper.

The guacamole
Mix together the avocado, tomato, chilli, coriander and chilli powder in a bowl. Stir in the lime juice.

The pico de gallo
Place the onion, chilli, lime juice and tomato in a bowl and mix well to combine.

cheesy potatopies

If you can, use fresh curd cheese in this recipe – the slightly sharp flavour is brilliant inside pastry. If not, choose a good quality, full fat cream cheese… avoid low-fat cheese at all costs, but you would anyway, wouldn't you?

Serves 4

150g potato, cubed
1 tbsp olive oil
1 onion, finely chopped
150g fresh ricotta
75g mature Lancashire cheese
salt and freshly ground black
   pepper
425g ready rolled puff pastry
1 free-range egg, beaten

Serve the cheese and potato pies with plenty of cooked vegetables (carrot, asparagus, mange-tout, spinach) tossed in butter and basil.

1 Cook the potato cubes in a large pan of salted boiling water for 10–12 minutes, until soft. Drain and leave to cool.

2 Meanwhile, heat the oil in a frying pan over a low heat. Fry the onion for 5–7 minutes, until soft. Remove from the heat and leave to cool a little.

3 In a bowl, combine the potato, ricotta, Lancashire cheese and onion. Mix together and season well with salt and pepper.

4 Preheat the oven to 200°C/400°C/gas mark 6.

5 On a lightly floured surface, roll out the pastry until it is a little thinner. Using a knife and a plate or saucer as a template cut out eight 15cm-diameter circles of pastry – you will need to fold and re-roll the excess pastry to make all eight circles.

6 Place four circles onto baking trays and spoon one quarter of the filling into the centre of each pastry piece, flattening slightly.

7 Brush the edges of the pastry with the beaten egg. Place another piece of pastry on top, press the edges to seal well and crimp around the edge with your fingers.

8 Brush the tops with more of the beaten egg and cook in the oven for 20 minutes, until the pastry is crisp and brown.

top tip:

If you make the bottom pastry circle a little bigger than the top, this will help prevent any of the filling from leaking out.

veggie chilli tacos

One of those light, girly Mexican beers with a lime wedge stuck in the top of the neck is great with these, but try a dark Mexican ale, like *negro modelo*.

Serves 4

2 tbsp vegetable oil
1 onion, finely chopped
1 garlic clove, crushed
3 celery stalks, finely chopped
200g brown cap or shiitake
    mushrooms, chopped
2 bird's eye chillies, chopped
50g tomato purée
1 tsp cocoa powder
100ml red wine
150ml vegetable stock
150g each of kidney, butter
    and soya beans
12 taco shells
150g mature Cheddar cheese,
    grated
200g soured cream
1 tbsp chopped coriander

Serve the veggie tacos on plates with cactus pickles or small pickled cucumbers.

1 Heat the oil in a frying pan over a medium heat. Fry the onion, garlic and celery for a few minutes, until soft but not browned.

2 Add the mushrooms and chillies and cook for a minute more, then add the tomato purée and cook for 2–3 minutes.

3 When the mushrooms are soft add the cocoa powder, red wine and stock and bring to the boil.

4 Reduce the heat and simmer for 15 minutes, then add the beans, and cook for 10 minutes more, until the beans are heated through and the sauce has reduced.

5 Warm the taco shells according to the packet instructions.

6 Fill each warmed taco shell with 2–3 tablespoons of the bean chilli. Top with the grated cheese, chopped coriander and a little sour cream.

top tip:

Adding a pinch of cocoa powder into the mix gives an extra depth of flavour. This works well with all chilli sauces and also with red wine sauces.

smoked haddock tempura
with salsa verde

I usually find tempura a bit dull – bland strips of veg deep fried in tasteless batter that never fails to disappoint. But try these guys – smoky, tasty, crispy and a sharp dipping sauce to finish it off.

Serves 4

For the tempura
125g plain flour
150ml ice-cold sparkling mineral water
1 free-range egg white
300g undyed smoked haddock, skinned
400ml vegetable oil

For the salsa verde
1 large bunch flat-leaf parsley
1 tbsp capers in vinegar
1 tbsp basil
1 tbsp rosemary
1 tbsp mint
2 anchovy fillets
75ml extra virgin olive oil
1 tsp white wine vinegar
1 garlic clove
salt and freshly ground black pepper

Serve the tempura on a large plate with lime wedges to squeeze over and a bowl of the salsa verde for dipping.

The tempura
1 Beat the flour and water together in a bowl.

2 Whisk the egg white until it forms stiff peaks. Gently fold it into the flour and water mixture until combined.

3 Cut the haddock into small strips and dip in the batter.

4 Pour the vegetable oil into a deep, heavy-bottomed saucepan, ensuring that it is no more than two-thirds full. Heat over a medium flame. When you can drop a breadcrumb into the oil and it sizzles and turns brown, it is hot enough to cook the battered fish strips. (It will be about 180°C/350°F, which you can check using a kitchen thermometer. Needless to say, be very careful with the hot oil and never leave it unattended.)

5 Place the fish pieces in the oil and deep-fry for 4–5 minutes, until the batter is crispy and golden brown and the fish is cooked. Carefully remove with a slotted spoon and drain on kitchen paper.

The salsa verde
1 In a food processor, blend the parsley, capers, basil, rosemary, mint, anchovy, olive oil, vinegar and garlic.

2 Season, to taste, with salt and pepper. (This is a dipping sauce, so you may also need to add a little more oil or vinegar.)

top tip:
Always use ice cold water when you make a batter. It will make it nice and crispy when you deep fry it.

salmon burgers
with basil and lime mayonnaise

Some things that are passed off as fish burgers are really no more than a square or round fish finger. Now, these are great – lots of flavour, great texture and they go down a treat with a few cold ones.

Serves 4
For the salmon burgers
600g skinless salmon,
    cut into chunks
75g white breadcrumbs
1 free-range egg white
1 shallot, finely chopped
1 tbsp chopped fresh basil
salt and freshly ground black
    pepper
2 tbsp vegetable oil
4 focaccia buns
1 Webb's lettuce, leaves
    separated
2 tomatoes, sliced
4 slices of smoked salmon

For the basil and lime mayonnaise
200g mayonnaise
2 tbsp finely chopped fresh basil
juice and zest 1 lime
1 garlic clove, crushed
salt and freshly ground black
    pepper

Serve each burger with a pile of big fat chips alongside and any leftover mayonnaise.

The salmon burgers
1 Place the salmon, breadcrumbs, egg white, shallot and basil in a food processor and pulse until combined but not puréed. Season with salt and pepper.

2 Turn out the mixture, divide it into four and shape each portion into a burger. Chill on a plate in the fridge for 30 minutes.

3 Heat the oil in a large frying pan over a medium heat. Fry the burgers for 3–5 minutes on each side, until golden-brown and cooked through.

4 Lightly griddle or toast the focaccia buns.

5 Place lettuce and tomato slices on one side of the focaccia buns. Place a burger on top and then a dollop of the mayonnaise (see recipe below). Top with a slice of smoked salmon and the bun lids.

The basil and lime mayonnaise
Combine the mayonnaise, basil, lime zest and juice and garlic in a bowl. Season, to taste, with salt and pepper.

top tip:
I like my salmon to be a little pink, but if you are worried about making sure the fish is cooked all the way through, cook the burgers in the oven at 180°C/350°F/gas mark 4 for 2–3 minutes after you've fried them.

2

treating your girlfriend

bacon, bran and
cinnamon muffins

american pancakes
with bacon

poached chicken salad

pasta primavera

tartare of salmon
and avocado

mushroom and caramelised
onion rarebit

new york smoked
salmon hash

posh beans on toast

crab noodle salad

roasted tomatoes and
mozzarella

coronation
chicken salad

poached salmon with
peas and chorizo

bacon bran and cinnamon muffins

Saturday tea-time, your team have won, so take advantage of your good mood and make a batch of these. Then, Sunday morning, feeling fragile, turn on *SFTW*, nip downstairs, warm them up, bring 'em up to bed with a brew and wait for your girlfriend's thank you.

Makes 6 large muffins

1 tbsp vegetable oil
75g smoked bacon lardons
25g bran
150ml milk
100g self-raising flour
100g wholemeal flour
2 tsp Demerara sugar
2 tsp baking powder
zest 1 lemon
1 tsp ground cinnamon
4 tbsp clear honey
75g butter
1 free-range egg
100ml natural yoghurt

Serve the muffins with a glass of fresh orange juice and a little butter to spread on them.

1 Heat the oil in a frying pan over a medium heat. Add the bacon and fry for 5–10 minutes, until browned and crispy. Remove from the heat and leave to cool a little.

2 Meanwhile, soak the bran in milk for 5 minutes.

3 Preheat the oven to 200°C/400°C/gas mark 6.

4 Sift the flours, sugar and baking powder into a bowl. Add the bacon, lemon and cinnamon.

5 In a small saucepan over a low heat melt the butter and heat the honey. Remove from the heat and beat in the egg, yoghurt and milk-soaked bran. Stir into the dry ingredients in the bowl.

6 Spoon the mixture into muffin cases and bake in the oven for 20–25 minutes, until golden-brown.

top tip:

Exchanging the natural yoghurt for 100ml buttermilk will produce lighter, fluffier muffins – although they won't be as healthy.

american pancakes with bacon

You can be a star in a U.S. drama making these. Rustle up the pancakes for your lady with the sun gently dappling through the kitchen window for full effect…you may want to think about teeth whitening, expensive hair cuts and gym sessions to be on the safe side.

Serves 2

100g self-raising flour
½ tsp bicarbonate of soda
20g caster sugar
30g unsalted butter, plus a knob, to serve
½ free-range egg
100ml milk
50g cottage cheese
100g blueberries (or raspberries or blackberries)
4 bacon rashers
little vegetable oil
maple syrup

Serve the pancakes with extra maple syrup to drizzle over.

1 Mix the flour, bicarbonate of soda and sugar together in a bowl.

2 In a small saucepan melt 20g butter over a low heat.

3 In a separate bowl combine the egg, melted butter, milk and cottage cheese. Add this to the flour mixture and mix together to make a batter.

4 Stir in the blueberries.

5 While you cook the pancakes, grill the bacon until it is crispy.

6 With a little butter and oil lightly grease a small frying pan and place over a medium heat. Spoon a small ladleful (about 2 tbsp) of the pancake batter into the pan and cook for a couple of minutes each side, or until golden and slightly puffed up. Repeat until you have used up all the batter.

7 Transfer the pancakes to serving plates, top with a dab of butter and two grilled rashers of bacon. Drizzle with maple syrup.

top tip:

For really perfect pancakes, make sure the texture of the pancake batter is thick and gloopy.

poached chicken salad
with red pepper dressing

Now I'm not saying that all girls love chicken, but they do. This one is soooo simple, but it looks like a) it's taken ages to make, b) you can cook, and c) you made it 'specially for her because you know chicken's her favourite.

Serves 2

For the poached chicken salad
2 chicken breasts
salt and freshly ground black pepper
75g soft goat's cheese
20ml double cream
8 sun-blushed tomatoes
4 basil leaves
bunch watercress

For the red pepper dressing
½ red pepper, roasted, skinned, chopped
1 tsp Dijon mustard
20ml white wine vinegar
100ml extra virgin olive oil
2 sprigs fresh tarragon, chopped

top tip:
If the dressing tastes too sharp, don't be afraid to add a little sugar to balance it out. This simple trick will work with most dressings.

Serve the salad with some crusty bread.

The poached chicken salad

1 Cut the mini-fillets off the chicken breasts and place to one side. Season the larger chicken breasts with salt and pepper.

2 Place the larger fillets between two sheets of cling film and, using a meat mallet or rolling pin, flatten out the meat as thinly as possible.

3 Place the reserved chicken mini-fillets, goat's cheese, cream, sun-blushed tomatoes and basil in a food processor and blend until smooth. Season, to taste, with salt and pepper.

4 Spread the chicken and goat's cheese mixture over each of the flattened chicken breasts, leaving a clear gap around the bottom edge of the meat.

5 Carefully roll the chicken up into a sausage shape and wrap it tightly in cling film. Wrap this in aluminium foil and seal the ends.

6 Fill a large pan with water, to a depth of about 10cm. Bring to the boil, reduce the heat and place the chicken parcels in the simmering water. Poach for 25 minutes, turning once.

7 Once poached, remove the chicken from its wrapping and pat dry with some kitchen paper. Cut the top and bottom ends off to tidy the roll, then cut into rounds.

8 Arrange the chicken pieces on a handful of the watercress and drizzle with the dressing (see recipe below).

The red pepper dressing
Place the red pepper, mustard, vinegar, oil and tarragon in a clean food processor and blend for 2–3 minutes until very smooth.

pasta
primavera

Whilst this actually means 'spring pasta', you can make it any time using lots of lovely, fresh, seasonal greens and good quality extra virgin olive oil, finished off with shavings of Parmesan – a winner.

Serves 2

200g fresh tagliolini
  (or 130g dried spaghettini)
100g asparagus, trimmed, halved
25g unsalted butter
1 garlic clove, crushed
75g frozen peas
75g frozen soya beans, defrosted
75g baby spinach
juice and zest 1 large lemon
1 tbsp mint leaves
1 tbsp basil leaves
1 tbsp dill
1 tbsp parsley leaves
salt and freshly ground black
  pepper

Serve the pasta topped with crushed toasted hazelnuts, Parmesan shavings and drizzled with olive oil.

1 Cook the pasta in a large pan of salted boiling water according to the packet instructions. Retaining a little of the cooking water, drain the pasta as soon as it is just cooked, but still a little firm.

2 Meanwhile, in another pan of boiling water quickly cook the asparagus for 2–3 minutes, until they are just cooked. Remove the spears and plunge into ice-cold water. This will stop them cooking further and retain their texture and colour.

3 Melt the butter in a large saucepan. Add the garlic and fry for one minute.

4 Add the asparagus, peas, soya beans and spinach and stir-fry for 1–2 minutes, until the spinach has started to wilt.

5 Add the cooked pasta and a little of its cooking water and stir to combine.

6 Stir in the lemon juice and zest and the herbs, and season, to taste, with salt and pepper.

top tip:
Adding a little of the pasta water to the final filling mixture will help to balance the overall flavour.

tartare of salmon and avocado
with prawns and pink grapefruit

Now, if this dish was your girlfriend you'd never want her to go. She's good to look at, tasty, your mum would approve, but deep down you know she's saucy.

Serves 2
6 king prawns, cooked, peeled
4–6 pink grapefruit segments

For the tartare of salmon and avocado
100ml fizzy pink wine
200g fresh salmon, skinned, finely chopped
juice and zest ½ lime
½ avocado, finely chopped
2 tsp dill
1 small shallot, finely chopped
salt and freshly ground black pepper

For the Thousand Island Dressing
100g mayonnaise
2 tsp tomato ketchup
1 tbsp brandy
splash Worcestershire sauce

Serve the tartare with any leftover Thousand Island Dressing on the side.

The tartare of salmon and avocado
1 Place the sparkling pink wine in a pan, bring to the boil and cook until the liquid has reduced to about 2 tablespoons. Remove from the heat and chill.

2 Mix the salmon, lime juice and zest, avocado, dill, shallot and reduced pink sparkling wine in a bowl. Season, to taste, with salt and pepper.

3 Spoon some of the tartare into the centre of each serving plate. (It's worth spending a bit of time arranging this into a neat round as it will look so much more impressive.) Arrange 3 prawns and 2 or 3 segments of pink grapefruit around the tartare and drizzle with a little of the dressing (see recipe below).

The Thousand Island Dressing
In a bowl combine the mayonnaise, tomato ketchup, brandy and Worcestershire sauce to make a smooth dressing.

top tip:
To peel an avocado easily, slice it in half and then run your thumb down the sides of the skin and the flesh will fall out. It must be ripe, though.

mushroom
and_caramelised
onion rarebit

There are lots of big strong flavours here, so you don't need a huge portion. As a lighter alternative you could use half ricotta cheese and half Cheddar.

Serves 2

75ml olive oil
1 large onion, finely sliced
2 very large or 4 medium field mushrooms, peeled, trimmed (stalks chopped and put back into mushrooms)
salt and freshly ground black pepper
1 garlic clove, crushed
15g unsalted butter
75g mature Cheddar or gruyére cheese, grated
½ tsp wholegrain mustard
1 small garlic clove, crushed
½ free-range egg, beaten

Serve the mushroom rarebit with warm crusty bread and a rocket, spinach and watercress salad.

1 Preheat the oven to 180°C/350°F/gas mark 4.

2 Heat 30ml oil in a small pan and fry the onions over a very low heat for about 30–40 minutes, stirring frequently, until they are soft, golden-brown and sweet.

3 Place the mushrooms in a baking dish and season with salt and pepper. Mix the crushed garlic with 45ml oil, brush over the mushrooms and top with a dot of butter. Cook in the oven for 10–12 minutes, until softened slightly.

4 Meanwhile, make the rarebit by combining the cheese, mustard, garlic and egg in a bowl.

5 Remove the mushrooms from the oven. Preheat the grill to its highest setting.

6 Into each mushroom spoon some of the rarebit mixture and caramelised onions. Press the mixture in well.

7 Place the mushrooms under the hot grill until the cheese bubbles, melts and browns.

top tip:

Never wash mushrooms as it will ruin their flavour and adds extra moisture that you don't want. If you have to clean them, then wipe them with a damp cloth.

new york
smoked
salmon
hash

This is a perfect Sunday brunch. If you only make one dish from this book, then this should be on the shortlist. Gorgeous smoked salmon with spuds and lots of other goodies – it's impossible not to have seconds.

Serves 2

For the smoked salmon hash

300g new potatoes
30g unsalted butter
½ small onion, finely sliced
1 tbsp chopped dill
1 tsp capers
75–100g smoked salmon,
   finely sliced
salt and freshly ground black
   pepper
4 rashers good quality, dry-cured
   smoked back bacon
2 free-range eggs

For the dressing

½ tbsp Dijon mustard
25ml white wine vinegar
juice of ½ lemon
100ml extra virgin olive oil
salt and freshly ground black
   pepper

top tip:

With capers, salmon and bacon, this dish can end up being rather salty. When you season everything in the frying pan, you might prefer to season with pepper only.

Serve the salmon hash with a little black pepper on top.

The smoked salmon hash

1 Cook the potatoes in a large pan of cold salted water for 10–12 minutes, until tender. Drain.

2 Meanwhile, melt the butter in a large frying pan over a medium heat. Fry the onion for 4–5 minutes, until soft.

3 Add the spuds to the onions and fry until they begin to soften and break down.

4 Add the dill, capers and smoked salmon and season well with salt and pepper. Stir to combine and cook until the salmon has turned pale pink.

5 Preheat the grill and then grill the bacon until it is crispy.

6 Heat a pan of water over a medium heat. Reduce the heat to low and gently break an egg into the water. Cook for 5 minutes, or until the white is firm. Carefully remove the egg with a slotted spoon, set aside and cover to keep warm while you poach the remaining egg.

7 Divide the potato mixture between two plates. Place two rashers of bacon alongside and a poached egg on top of the potato. Top with a little of the dressing (see recipe below).

The dressing
Place the mustard, vinegar, oil and lemon juice in a bowl and season with salt and pepper. Whisk together to form a smooth vinaigrette. (If you don't use it all, this dressing keeps well in a screw-top jar in the fridge.)

posh beans on toast

Surprisingly, this is a pretty healthy dish and so much tastier than beans from a tin. In fact, once you've made them you'll never return to the tin again…maybe.

Serves 2

1 tbsp vegetable oil.
1 onion, chopped
1 garlic clove, chopped
1 tbsp of tomato purée
400g can chopped tomatoes
100ml hot vegetable stock
salt and freshly ground black
   pepper
100g bacon lardons
400g canned mixed white beans
   (butter beans, cannellini beans
   etc.) rinsed, drained
4 slices brioche
unsalted butter (for the brioche)

Serve the brioche with a thin smear of marmite (optional) and garnish the beans with a sprig of thyme.

1 Heat the vegetable oil in a frying pan over a low heat. Add the onion and garlic and fry for 4–5 minutes, until soft.

2 Stir in the tomato purée and cook, stirring often, for 5 minutes.

3 Add the chopped tomatoes and vegetable stock and bring to the boil. Reduce the heat and simmer for 40 minutes. It will have the consistency of a thick-ish sauce. (Stir occasionally to prevent it burning.)

4 Using a hand-held blender, blend the sauce. Pass it through a sieve to remove any bits. Season well with salt and pepper.

5 In a saucepan, fry the bacon lardons until crisp. Add the beans, then the tomato sauce, stir and heat through. Cover and simmer gently for a further 5–10 minutes, stirring occasionally, until it has thickened and become syrupy.

6 Meanwhile, toast the brioche slices and spread with butter. Serve two slices of brioche each, topped with the beans.

top tip:

Always rinse canned beans well. You must get rid of the starch and any chemical residue from the tin.

crab noodle salad
with nuoc cham

If you've ever been to Thailand or the Far East then this dish will send you right back there – aromatic with a superb chilli kick.

Serves 2

For the crab noodle salad

100g fine rice noodles
150g crab meat, cooked
½ red onion, very finely sliced
1 tbsp finely chopped coriander
2 lime leaves, finely sliced
½ red pepper, finely chopped
½ cucumber, seeds removed, finely diced
salt and freshly ground black pepper

For the nuoc cham

1 small red chilli
1 garlic clove
juice 2 limes
1 lemon grass stalk, finely chopped
40ml rice vinegar

This will sound a little bizarre, but if you are worried about the spiciness, serve this with a bowl of raw, chopped white cabbage – the best thing to counteract the heat.

The crab noodle salad

1 Soak the rice noodles in very hot water for 5 minutes, or until they are soft. Drain and set aside.

2 Place the crab meat, onion, coriander, lime leaves, red pepper and cucumber in a large bowl and mix together well. Season, to taste, with salt and pepper.

The nuoc cham

Combine the chilli, garlic, lime juice, lemon grass and vinegar in a food processor and blend to form a smooth paste. (If it seems a little thick add a splash of water.)

To assemble the salad

1 Mix a little of the nuoc cham dressing into the noodles.

2 Fold half of the crab mixture into the noodles. Wrap half the noodles around a large fork and gently place into a small bowl to make a 'nest'. Repeat with a second bowl.

3 Spoon some of the dressing over each noodle nest and top with more crab and a little more dressing.

top tip:
Blend the dry ingredients first to break them down before adding the liquids. This will ensure a smooth, even paste.

roasted
tomatoes and
mozzarella
with lemon-chilli dressing

It might seem odd to make half of this dish so far in advance, but make loads of the dressing and it'll keep in a jar in the fridge, and double up on the tomatoes and store them, covered in oil in the fridge, until next time. Once you've tasted the end result you'll realise it's more than worth the effort.

Serves 2

For the tomato salad
150g sea salt
8 plum tomatoes, halved lengthways
handful of watercress or rocket salad
150g buffalo mozzarella ball, roughly torn
8–10 Kalamata olives
4 basil leaves

For the lemon-chilli dressing
3 unwaxed lemons, halved
2 tsp sugar
2 tsp sea salt
1 small garlic clove
2 red chillies, chopped
1 tsp whole black peppercorns
olive oil, to top up the jar

Serve the salad with a hunk of focaccia to soak up all the lovely dressing.

The tomato salad

1 Preheat the oven to its coolest setting. Sprinkle the sea salt onto a baking tray. Place the tomatoes cut-side up on the salt.

2 Place the tray of tomatoes on the bottom shelf of the oven for at least 4 hours. (The salt will take all the moisture from the tomatoes and dry them out.)

3 Arrange the salad leaves on two plates. Divide the tomatoes, mozzarella and olives between the plates and scatter basil leaves over the top. Drizzle with some of the lemon chilli dressing (see recipe below), making sure you get a bit of the chilli.

The lemon-chilli dressing

1 Place the lemons, sugar, salt, garlic, chillies and peppercorns into a bowl and stir to combine, pressing the lemons slightly with a wooden spoon to extract a little lemon juice. Transfer to a vacuum-sealed jar.

2 Top up the jar with olive oil and leave ideally for a week but at least 24 hours.

top tip:
Instead of chopping the chillies for the dressing, you can prick them and they will release just as much flavour – great if you want to make chilli-flavoured vodka.

coronation chicken salad

This is the best thing about the monarchy – the invention of Coronation Chicken back in 1953. Good versions of this make the best sandwiches and, in this case, a mighty fine salad.

Serves 2

200g new potatoes
4 spring onions, finely chopped
1 tsp white wine vinegar
1 tbsp extra virgin olive oil
salt and freshly ground black
   pepper
100g mayonnaise
50g smooth curry paste
   (you might need to soften
   it with a little hot water)
20g sultanas
15g flaked, toasted almonds
2 small ready-to-eat
   chicken breasts
1 tbsp coriander leaves
bunch watercress

Serve the chicken with a hunk of walnut bread to mop up the sauce.

1 Cook the spuds in boiling salted water for 15 minutes, until they are nearly soft.

2 While they are still hot, cut the potatoes into quarters and place in a bowl with the spring onions, vinegar and oil. Toss together well (the warm spuds will absorb the dressing). Season, to taste, with salt and pepper. Leave to cool.

3 In another bowl, mix the mayonnaise with the curry paste.

4 When the potatoes have cooled, combine the mayonnaise mixture with the spuds. Stir in the sultanas and almonds.

5 Slice the chicken thickly, across the face of the breast.

6 Add the chicken and coriander to the potato mixture and stir gently to combine.

7 Place a handful of watercress on each plate and serve a generous portion of the chicken salad on top.

top tip:

A good way to save money is to buy a whole chicken and cut off the breasts for this dish. You can freeze the leftover chicken and use it in other dishes.

poached salmon
with peas and chorizo

This is another dead simple dish that looks a lot harder than it actually is. The flavours are superb – delicate poached salmon brought to life by the smoky chorizo, supported by the king of the store cupboard, the garden pea.

Serves 2

juice 1 small lemon
6 white peppercorns
100ml white wine
1 tsp sea salt
2 x 125g salmon fillets
75g chorizo, cut into bite-sized chunks
100ml dry sherry
200g frozen peas
1 tbsp fresh dill
2–3 tbsp extra virgin olive oil
sea salt and freshly ground black pepper

Serve each poached salmon fillet on top of a large handful of mixed salad leaves. Drizzle generously with the peas and chorizo dressing.

1 Place half the lemon juice, the peppercorns, white wine, 100ml water and sea salt into a deep frying pan over a medium heat and bring to a steady simmer.

2 Carefully slide in the salmon fillets (top up the poaching liquid with more water if necessary, to ensure the fillets are covered). Bring the liquid back up to a simmer, remove from the heat and leave for about 25 minutes, until the fish is just cooked through.

3 Remove the salmon from the liquid and leave to cool.

4 Meanwhile, heat a clean frying pan until it is very hot, then chuck in the chorizo. Let it crisp very slightly, then add the sherry. Simmer until the liquid has reduced by about two thirds.

5 Remove from the heat and add the remaining lemon juice.

6 Add the peas, dill and olive oil and season, to taste, with salt and pepper. Stir well to combine and warm through.

top tip:

To poach a whole salmon (too large for a pan), wrap it in cling film, then in foil and put it in the dishwasher on a standard rinse for as long as it would need to poach in a saucepan for.

3

food to share

salmon sushi rolls

chicken koftas with
yoghurt dressing

home-made flatbread
and spicy houmous

breakfast burritos

huevos rancheros
(ranch eggs with kale)

almond rolled
goat's cheese

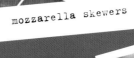
mozzarella skewers

seafood bhajis
with yoghurt dressing

tuna and ricotta
fritters

pork pies

prawn dim sum

pollack goujons

salmon sushi rolls

Hands up if you think sushi means 'raw fish'. Thought so, most of you. Well, it actually means 'vinegared rice'. It is also incredibly easy to make and brilliant for parties, or just for a bunch of friends.

Serves 6
For the sushi rolls
150g sushi rice, rinsed
   thoroughly, drained
salt
25g sugar
50ml rice wine vinegar
4 sheets of dried nori (roasted
   and rolled seaweed)
50-75g wasabi paste
½ cucumber, peeled, deseeded
   cut into batons
½ red pepper, deseeded,
   cut into batons
200g fresh salmon, cut into strips
   about 0.5cm thick

For the dipping sauce
100ml rice vinegar
75g sugar
1 small red chilli, finely chopped

top tip:
Before cutting the sushi roll, chill it in the fridge for 30 minutes. This will soften the seaweed a little, making it easier to cut.

Serve the sushi rolls on a large platter with a bowl of the dipping sauce, extra wasabi paste, soy sauce and pickled red ginger.

The sushi rolls
1 Place the rice in a saucepan with 250ml cold water and bring to the boil. Cover and simmer for 15 minutes, until all the water is absorbed and the rice is tender. Remove from the heat, stir in the sugar and vinegar, leave covered and allow to cool.

2 When the rice is cool, transfer it to a bowl, season with salt and mix together well.

3 Lay out the nori sheets and spread a little of the wasabi paste onto each.

4 Place a line of the rice mixture about 2.5cm wide a little way in from the bottom edge of each nori sheet.

5 Press the cucumber batons, pepper batons and salmon strips into the rice along each nori sheet. Roll up tightly.

6 With a sharp knife cut the rolls into 4cm-long pieces, discarding the uneven ends.

The dipping sauce
In a small saucepan heat the vinegar, sugar and chilli until the sugar dissolves, stirring occasionally.

chicken koftas
with yoghurt dressing

Koftas, meatballs and the like always need to leave a lasting taste impression, otherwise you may as well just fry a bit of mince. The seasoning in the actual koftas, and also in the yoghurt dressing, means you probably shouldn't make these if you're after a snog.

Serves 4
For the koftas
1 tbsp olive oil
1 onion, finely chopped
1 garlic clove, crushed
1 bird's eye chilli, chopped
½ tsp cinnamon
½ tsp nutmeg
½ tsp paprika
½ tsp cumin
450g chicken mince
salt and freshly ground black
    pepper
50g butter
juice of ½ lemon

For the yoghurt dressing
200g Greek yoghurt
2 tbsp chopped mint
½ cucumber, seeds removed,
    grated
juice of ½ lime

Serve the koftas with flatbreads, the yoghurt dressing to dip, a lemon wedge and garnished with mint leaves.

The koftas
1 Heat the oil in a frying pan over a medium heat and gently fry the onion and garlic for 5–6 minutes until soft. Remove from the heat and leave to cool a little.

2 Place the chicken mince in a large bowl. Add the fried onion and garlic.

3 Stir in the chilli, cinnamon, nutmeg, paprika and cumin. Season with salt and pepper and mix well.

4 Preheat the grill to its highest setting. In a small saucepan melt the butter.

5 Carefully shape the mixture into twelve walnut-sized balls and thread three balls onto a wooden skewer, leaving a small gap between each ball to ensure they cook evenly. Repeat with the remaining balls and skewers.

6 Place the skewers under the grill for 8–10 minutes, turning them regularly and basting with the melted butter and lemon juice. (Let them go crispy before you first baste them.) When they are golden-brown and cooked through, remove from the grill.

The yoghurt dressing
In a bowl combine the mint, cucumber and lime juice with the yoghurt. Mix together well.

top tip:
Soak the skewers in water for a few minutes, so that they don't burn when they are under the grill.

home-made flatbread and spicy houmous

If you've shied away from making bread, then starting with a flatbread will break you in gently. It doesn't matter if they don't rise, in fact you don't want them to. Breaking bread together is a cool way to make friends, break the ice and get things moving.

Serves 6

For the flatbread

1 tsp coriander seeds
250ml natural yoghurt
1½ tsp dried yeast
550g strong plain flour, plus extra for dusting
1 tbsp salt
2 tbsp vegetable oil, plus extra for brushing

For the spicy houmous

400g tinned chickpeas, drained, rinsed
4 garlic cloves
50g tahini paste
juice of 3 lemons
100g spicy red pepperdew peppers
salt and freshly ground black pepper
2–3 tbsp olive oil

top tip:

If the houmous is too runny, add more chickpeas; if it seems too thick, then add more oil.

Serve the flatbread on a plate with bowls of olive oil and the houmous, garnished with olives, to dip into.

The flatbread

1 Toast the coriander seeds in a dry frying pan over a medium heat for 1–2 minutes, until they turn golden-brown. Using a mortar and pestle, lightly crush the seeds. Don't turn them into powder, but don't leave them tooth-breaking size.

2 Place the crushed seeds in a saucepan with 100ml water and bring to the boil. Then put to one side.

3 Place the yoghurt in a bowl and add the yeast. Pour the coriander seeds and water into the yoghurt mixture and stir well.

4 Add the flour, salt and oil and, using your hands, combine well and form a soft dough. Cover the bowl and leave in a warm place to prove for 25–45 minutes. It should have nearly doubled in size. (It doesn't have to be somewhere warm, but it helps.)

5 Turn the dough out onto a lightly floured surface and knead it gently for a few minutes until it is smooth and elastic.

6 Divide the dough into six, then shape each portion into a little ball. Roll each ball out to 10–12.5cm circles.

7 Heat a griddle or shallow pan. Brush each circle of dough with a little oil and cook for about 40–50 seconds on each side, until golden-brown all over.

The spicy houmous

Place the chickpeas, garlic, tahini paste, lemon juice and peppers in a food processor. Season with salt and pepper and blend until smooth. With the motor still running, add a steady stream of oil, to loosen the mixture.

breakfast
burritos

Feel free to add bacon, sausages, mushrooms or even black pudding to this – just don't forget the Hot Sauce.

Serves 4

2 red peppers, quartered, seeded
4 free-range eggs
4 tbsp milk
salt and freshly ground black pepper
1 tbsp butter
6 pepperdew peppers, finely chopped
handful baby spinach
1 tbsp olive oil
squeeze lemon juice
Jamaican Hot Pepper Sauce
4 soft corn or flour tortillas
75g mature cheddar, grated

Serve the tortillas with more Jamaican Hot Pepper Sauce.

1 Preheat the oven to 200°C/400°F/gas mark 6. Cook the red peppers for about 15 minutes, until they have softened.

2 Meanwhile, place the eggs and milk in a bowl. Season with salt and pepper and whisk together until combined.

3 In a non-stick frying pan melt the butter. When it begins to foam add the egg mixture.

4 Without stirring, cook the eggs until they are just beginning to set. When they have set, push the egg gently towards the centre of the pan with a spatula.

5 Continue to do this until the egg mixture has set, then flip the mixture over and remove from the heat.

6 Remove the peppers from the oven and place in a polythene bag for a few minutes, to soften the skins.

7 Place the pepperdew peppers and spinach in a bowl and mix together well with the oil, lemon juice, 1–2 tbsp Hot Pepper Sauce and a little salt and pepper.

8 Peel and chop the roasted peppers and add to the spinach mix.

9 Warm the tortillas according to the packet instructions.

10 Place a warmed tortilla on each plate. Line the edge of each tortilla with some cheese and top with the spinach and pepper mixture. Add a couple of spoonfuls of the eggs and roll up the tortilla tightly.

top tip:

If you find the scrambled eggs are cooking too quickly, remove the pan from the heat and move the eggs into the centre of the pan, so that they cook from the outside in.

huevos rancheros
(ranch eggs with kale)

Whenever I go to the States I have to have this, it's just so damn tasty. I mean what's not to like? Eggs, tortillas, salsa and chilli sauce…make it for all your mates NOW!

Serves 4

3 kale leaves, finely chopped
1 onion, finely chopped
1 green pepper, finely chopped
1 red pepper, finely chopped
1 small bird's eye chilli, finely chopped
1 courgette, finely chopped
1 garlic clove, finely chopped
150ml tomato passata
salt and freshly ground black pepper
1 tbsp oil
4 knobs of butter
8 free-range eggs

Serve the eggs with a pile of warm tortillas and some hot chilli sauce. Dip the warm tortillas into the yolks and dare yourself to overdo the chilli sauce.

1 Place the kale, onion, green and red peppers, chilli, courgette, garlic and passata in a bowl. Season with salt and pepper and mix together well. (You may not need to use all of the passata. The vegetables should be bound by the sauce, not swimming in it.)

2 Heat the oil in a lidded frying pan over a medium heat. Add a quarter of the salsa mixture and warm through.

3 Make a hole in the middle of the salsa and melt a knob of butter in the gap. Break two eggs into this space then put the lid on the pan and cook for 3–4 minutes. The dish is ready when the eggs are cooked into the salsa and the whites are firm.

4 Slide the eggs and salsa onto a large serving plate and keep warm while you repeat this process three times with the remaining salsa and eggs.

top tip:
To control the heat of chillies take out the seeds, the heat is in these little things.

almond rolled goat's cheese

If you're going to make things to share they need to be sociable in the way you eat them. Like bread, these babies are dead easy to make in bigger quantities. Fry them in slightly cooler oil so the cheese has chance to melt.

Serves 4

For the roasted beetroot
250g fresh beetroot, trimmed
salt and freshly ground black
    pepper
75ml olive oil
1 tbsp balsamic vinegar

For the goat's cheese balls
400ml vegetable oil
200g soft goat's cheese
75g plain flour
200g flaked almonds

For the dressing
80g fresh basil leaves
50g smoked almonds
1 garlic clove
50g Parmesan cheese
60ml olive oil

Serve the cheese balls in lettuce leaves. Place a few cubes of beetroot and a little of the dressing around the cheese .

The roasted beetroot

1 Preheat the oven to 200°C/400°F/gas mark 6.

2 Peel the beetroot and cut into cubes. Spread the cubes out in a baking dish. Season well with salt and pepper and drizzle with olive oil. Roast for about 30 minutes, until soft.

3 Remove the beetroot from the oven and while it is still hot place in a bowl. Drizzle with the balsamic vinegar and stir to coat.

The goat's cheese balls

1 Pour the vegetable oil into a deep, heavy-bottomed saucepan, ensuring that it is no more than two-thirds full. Heat over a medium flame. When you can drop a breadcrumb into the oil and it sizzles and turns brown, it is hot enough to cook the goat's cheese balls. (The oil will be about 180°C/350°F. Needless to say, be very careful with the hot oil and never leave it unattended.)

2 Meanwhile, divide the goat's cheese into eight equal-sized pieces and roll each piece into a ball.

3 Place the flour in a shallow bowl and roll the balls through the flour to cover.

4 Spread the almonds on a plate and roll the cheese balls through them, pressing the flaked almonds into the cheese. (You will need to press the almonds into the cheese quite firmly so that they stick. Don't worry if the almonds break up a bit.)

5 Carefully place the cheese balls in the hot oil and deep fry for about 30 seconds–1 minute, until golden-brown all over. Remove the balls with a slotted spoon and drain on kitchen paper.

top tip:

Goat's cheese can dry out, making it hard to get the almonds to stick. Rub oil onto your hands to act as a glue and press them in.

The dressing

Place the basil, smoked almonds, garlic, Parmesan and olive oil in a processor and blend until smooth.

mozzarella skewers
with tomato and anchovy sauce

This is one of Tim's faves. Don't be afraid of the anchovies used in the sauce – they really help to bring out the best in the mozzarella.

Serves 4

For the tomato and anchovy sauce

10 canned anchovies, rinsed, drained, finely chopped
200g cherry tomatoes, halved
salt and freshly ground black pepper
100ml olive oil
juice of ½ lemon
1 tbsp fresh thyme
1 garlic clove, crushed
1 tbsp pine nuts
2 tbsp red wine vinegar

For the mozzarella skewers

450g buffalo mozzarella, torn into pieces (about 50g each)
50g plain flour, well seasoned with salt and freshly ground black pepper
2 free-range eggs, beaten
75–100g fresh breadcrumbs
200ml vegetable oil

Place a spoonful of the tomato and anchovy sauce onto each plate or into a small bowl and serve with a mozzarella skewer on top.

The tomato and anchovy sauce

1 Preheat the oven to 180°C/350°F/gas mark 4.

2 Place the tomatoes, cut-side up, in a shallow baking dish.

3 Lay the anchovies on top and season with salt and pepper. Drizzle over the olive oil and roast in the oven for 20 minutes, until they have softened.

4 Once the tomatoes are cooked add the lemon juice, thyme, garlic, pine nuts and red wine vinegar and mix together gently.

The mozzarella skewers

1 Place the seasoned flour in a shallow bowl and roll the cheese pieces through it, to cover.

2 Dip the floured cheese in the beaten egg and then roll through the breadcrumbs to cover completely.

3 Heat the oil in a deep frying pan until it's almost smoking hot. Carefully add the cheese balls and fry for about 5 minutes, turning regularly, until they are crisp and golden-brown all over. Remove with a slotted spoon and drain on kitchen paper.

4 Thread three balls each onto wooden skewers.

top tip:
When you thread the mozzarella balls onto the skewers, leave a little space between them so that they don't melt into each other and become a mush.

seafood
bhajis
with yoghurt dressing

Depending on how you want to share these, I'd change the size of the bhajis. If there's only a few of you, then make 'em the size of small tennis balls, but if it's party time then little ones (just a mouthful) will obviously go further.

Serves 4
For the seafood bhajis
300g gram flour (chickpea flour)
1 green chilli, finely chopped
400ml vegetable oil, plus 2 tbsp
1 large onion, sliced
100g king prawns
100g salmon, cut into
   small pieces
100g haddock, cut into
   small pieces

For the yoghurt dressing
250g natural yoghurt
2 tbsp mint
½ lime, squeezed

Serve the bhajis with the yoghurt dressing, sprinkled with a little coriander, and mango chutney.

The seafood bhajis
1 Place the flour in a large bowl and gradually whisk in 175–250ml water. Keep beating until you have a consistency similar to pouring cream, then add the chilli.

2 Heat 2 tbsp vegetable oil in a pan and fry the onion over a medium heat, until soft but not coloured. Remove with a slotted spoon and drain well on kitchen paper.

3 In a bowl combine the prawns and fish with the cooked onion.

4 Pour the 400ml vegetable oil in a deep, heavy-bottomed saucepan, ensuring that it is no more than two-thirds full. Heat over a medium flame. When you can drop a breadcrumb into the oil and it sizzles and turns brown, it is hot enough to cook the bhajis. (The oil will be about 180°C/350°F. Needless to say, be very careful with the hot oil and never leave it unattended.)

5 Using a tablespoon dip even amounts of the fish mixture in the batter and then place carefully in the hot oil. Cook for 8–10 minutes, until crisp and golden and cooked through. Carefully remove the bhajis with a slotted spoon and drain well on some kitchen paper.

The yoghurt dressing
Mix the yoghurt with the mint and lime juice to make a dressing.

top tip:
If you have some herbs left over, store them by laying them flat in a freezer bag and placing in the freezer until you next need them.

tuna
and ricotta
fritters
with tartare sauce

The smell of these when they're cooking makes me salivate. It's a bit of a chip shop smell, but in a nice way. I strongly recommend that you make about twice as many as you need because you'll eat half of them before your guests even get near them.

Serves 4–6
For the tuna and ricotta fritters
400ml vegetable oil
450g potatoes, unpeeled
200g canned tuna in olive oil, drained
100g ricotta, drained for at least 2 hours
2 free-range eggs, separated
1 tbsp marjoram
salt and freshly ground pepper
100g plain flour
2 tbsp parsley, chopped
120g breadcrumbs

For the tartare sauce
150g mayonnaise
1 tsp English mustard
6 small gherkins
1 tsp capers, in vinegar
1 garlic clove crushed
1 tbsp chopped parsley
juice of 1 lime
salt and freshly ground black pepper

top tip:
Wrap the ricotta in a muslin cloth and squeeze it. This will stop the balls being sloppy.

Serve the fritters sprinkled with a little lemon zest and a bowl of the tartare sauce to dip into.

The tuna and ricotta fritters
1 Cut the potatoes into chunks. Cook them in boiling salted water for 20 minutes, until soft. Drain, peel and mash in a large bowl.

2 Add the tuna, ricotta, egg yolks and marjoram and season well with salt and pepper. Chill the mixture for 30 minutes to firm up.

3 With floured hands, mould the potato and tuna mixture into golf-ball sized balls. Place the flour in a shallow bowl and roll the potato and tuna balls through the flour to coat. Place the egg whites in a clean bowl and beat lightly. Mix together the chopped parsley and breadcrumbs in another bowl. Dip the floured tuna balls into the beaten egg whites and then into the parsley and breadcrumb mixture.

4 Pour the vegetable oil in a deep, heavy-bottomed saucepan, ensuring that it is no more than two-thirds full. Heat over a medium flame. When you can drop a breadcrumb into the oil and it sizzles and turns brown, it is hot enough to cook the fritters. (It will be about 180°C/350°F, which you can check using a kitchen thermometer. Needless to say, be very careful with the hot oil and never leave it unattended.)

5 Deep-fry the tuna balls for about 4 minutes, until golden. You may need to cook them in batches. Carefully remove with a slotted spoon and drain on kitchen paper.

The tartare sauce
Mix together the mayonnaise, mustard, gherkins, capers, garlic, parsley and lime juice. Season, to taste, with salt and pepper.

pork
pies

Dom Joly made these on the show and seemed disappointed that that was 'all' we were making. However, once he started making the pastry (which is very therapeutic) he was hooked on the art of pie making…and you will be, too.

Serves 4
For the filling
400g pork shoulder, diced
150g lean smoked bacon
1 tbsp chopped fresh sage
1 tbsp finely chopped rosemary
½ tsp ground nutmeg
½ tsp allspice
2 tsp anchovy essence
   or 1 fresh salted anchovy,
   finely chopped
salt and freshly ground black
   pepper

For the pastry
400g plain flour
salt and freshly ground black
   pepper
40ml whole milk
150g lard, cubed
1 free-range egg yolk, beaten

top tip:
It is better to use a proper pork pie tin for this, but if you don't have one, you can make eight smaller pork pies in a muffin tin and serve two each.

Serve quarters of pie with pickled onions and a beer.

1 Preheat the oven to 180°C/350°F/gas mark 4.

2 In a food processor, pulse half the pork shoulder and half the bacon until it forms a coarse mince. In a bowl, combine with the rest of the meat, the sage, rosemary, nutmeg, allspice and anchovy essence. Season with salt and pepper.

The pastry
1 Sift the flour and salt and pepper into a large bowl.

2 Place the milk, 50ml warm water and lard in a small pan and bring slowly to a simmer, until all the lard has melted. Bring to the boil and then pour onto the flour mixture. Mix well with a wooden spoon to create a dough.

3 Turn out onto a floured surface and knead until smooth. Use whilst still warm or the pastry will start to harden up.

To assemble the pie
1 Set aside, covered, one-quarter of the dough for the lid. Roll the rest of the dough out flat then press the dough into a pork pie tin.

2 Spoon the meat filling into the pastry-lined tin.

3 From the leftover pastry, roll out a lid slightly larger than the tin.

4 Brush the pastry lid with a little beaten egg. Place the lid on top of the meat mixture and press down to seal the edges. Cut a small hole in the top to let out the steam while the pie cooks.

5 Cook in the oven for 45–55 minutes, until the pastry is golden-brown and the meat is cooked through.

6 Remove from the oven and remove the sides of the tin. Brush with the remaining egg and return to the oven, increase the heat to 200°C/400°F/gas mark 6. Cook for a further 10 minutes until nicely golden brown. Cool before serving.

prawn dim sum

Confession time: I'm not the biggest fan of dim sum, because it can be very bland. So, these little babies have some extra little bits of veg to give a more interesting texture and flavour.

Makes 30 dim sum

For the dim sum

75g squid, cleaned, finely chopped

275g raw king prawns, shelled, cleaned, chopped

1 carrot, finely diced

30g shiitake mushrooms, finely chopped

40g cornflour, mixed with 40ml water to make a paste

3 tbsp sesame oil

½ tsp sugar

salt and freshly ground black pepper

30 dim sum wrappers (from Asian supermarkets)

For the dipping sauce

50ml light soy sauce

50ml dark soy sauce

1 tsp hot chilli oil

½ tsp sugar

1 garlic clove, crushed

1 tsp ginger, crushed

top tip:

If you don't own a steamer, place a large, deep plate over a pan of boiling water. Place the dim sum in it and cover with another deep plate, upside down, to make a lid. The dim sum will steam inside the plates.

Serve the dim sum with some baby herbs and cress or an Asian leaf salad, with the dipping sauce alongside.

The dim sum

1 Using your hands mix the squid, prawns, carrot, mushrooms, cornflour paste, sesame oil, sugar and salt and pepper together to form a paste.

2 Lay a dim sum wrapper in the palm of your hand and brush the edges with water. Spoon about 2 teaspoons of the mixture into the middle of the dim sum wrapper, then pinch at the top to make a pirate's hat shape. Repeat with the rest of the mixture and dim sum wrappers.

3 Place the dim sum on an oiled plate. (Any oil is fine. This will prevent the dim sum from sticking to the steamer as they cook.) Place the dim sum in a steamer and cook for 6–7 minutes, until the prawns are cooked.

The dipping sauce

Combine the dark and light soy sauce, chilli oil, sugar, garlic and ginger in a bowl.

pollack goujons
with tamarind sauce

Imagine if that well-known sea captain were to hold a dinner party and wanted to be a bit posher than his fish fingers. Well, he'd make these for all the sailors. 'Ah-ha, me hearties.'

Serves 4

For the pollack goujons
400ml vegetable oil
125g breadcrumbs
55g desiccated coconut
salt and freshly ground black
  pepper
250g pollack, skinned and cut
  into strips
55g plain flour
2 free-range eggs, beaten

For the tamarind sauce
200ml tamarind concentrate
75ml honey
1 tbsp light soy sauce
2 garlic cloves, crushed
1 tbsp grated ginger
juice 2 limes

Serve the pollack goujons with a bowl of the tamarind dipping sauce and a beer. Garnish the goujons with lime wedges and scatter with chopped parsley.

The pollack goujons

1 Pour the vegetable oil in a deep, heavy-bottomed saucepan, ensuring that it is no more than two-thirds full. Heat over a medium flame. When you can drop a breadcrumb into the oil and it sizzles and turns brown, it is hot enough to cook the goujons. (It will be about 180°C/350°F, which you can check using a kitchen thermometer. Needless to say, be very careful with the hot oil and never leave it unattended.)

2 Meanwhile, combine the breadcrumbs and dessicated coconut in a shallow bowl.

3 Season the fish all over with salt and pepper and then dredge in the flour, to coat.

4 Dip the floured fish in the beaten egg, then dip in the breadcrumb mixture, to cover.

5 Place the coated fish strips in the hot oil and deep-fry for 4–5 minutes, or until crisp and golden and the fish is cooked through. Carefully remove with a slotted spoon and drain on kitchen paper.

The tamarind sauce

Place the tamarind concentrate, honey, soy sauce, garlic and ginger in a pan. Bring to the boil, simmer for 1 minute, while the sauce thickens, then remove from the heat. Stir in the lime juice.

top tip:
If you want to make your own breadcrumbs don't toast the bread, put it in the bottom of the oven on a low heat and let it dry out.

4

the olds round for brunch

meat feast calzone

baked macaroni and
meatballs

smoked cheese sausages

beetroot rosti with
smoked salmon

spicy puy lentil bake

smoked mackerel
kedgeree

smoked cheese
and potato cakes

haddock and
sweetcorn chowder

breakfast frittata

chicken
stroganoff pie

pork loin with fig
and balsamic vinegar

classic chicken
caesar salad

baked
macaroni
and
meatballs

Imagine that your folks are Italian, imagine that they taste this macaroni and meatballs. They start to cry because the taste reminds them of being in Italy, your mum cups your face in her hands and kisses you. Your dad (did I mention he's rich?) buys you a Maserati.

Serves 4
For the cheese sauce
750ml whole milk
2 bay leaves
30g unsalted butter
40g plain flour
200g mature Cheddar or gruyère, grated
1 tsp English mustard
salt and freshly ground black pepper

For the meatballs
2 tbsp olive oil
½ onion, finely chopped
1 garlic clove, crushed
1 tsp dried oregano
250g minced rump steak
salt and freshly ground black pepper
2 tbsp vegetable oil

For the macaroni
150g macaroni
2 tbsp vegetable oil
4 shallots, sliced
20 cherry tomatoes, halved
12 sun-blushed tomatoes
1 tsp dried oregano
2 tbsp grated Parmesan

Serve the macaroni and meatballs with a green salad.

The cheese sauce
1 Pour the milk into a pan, add the bay leaves and place over a medium heat. Bring to scalding point then remove from the heat.

2 In another pan melt the butter, stir in the flour and cook for 3 minutes – don't let it brown.

3 Remove the bay leaves from the milk and add a little of the milk to the flour. Mix with a wooden spoon to combine and cook out a little over a low heat. Repeat the process, gradually adding more milk, until the mixture has formed a smooth paste.

4 Add the rest of the milk and bring to the boil, stirring all the time. Reduce the heat and simmer for 3 minutes.

5 Remove from the heat and stir in the cheese, mustard and salt and pepper. Set to one side.

The meatballs
1 Heat the olive oil in a frying pan and fry the onion, garlic and oregano for a few minutes, until soft. Remove from the heat and leave to cool.

2 Place the onion mixture in a bowl and add the mince. Season well with salt and pepper and mix to combine. Roll the mince mixture into 2.5cm meatballs.

3 Heat the vegetable oil in a clean frying pan over a medium heat. Fry the meatballs, turning occasionally, for about 2–3 minutes until they are brown all over and cooked through.

To assemble the macaroni and meatballs
1 Cook the pasta according to the packet instructions until it is just tender. Drain well.

2 Preheat the oven to 200°C/400°F/gas mark 6.

top tip:

When you're making the white sauce, don't add any milk to the roux (the flour and butter) until it starts to bubble. That means the flour will have been cooked out.

3 Heat the vegetable oil in a large frying pan and fry the shallots for 1–2 minutes, until soft.

4 Add the cooked pasta, tomatoes, meatballs and white sauce (you may need to add a little milk to loosen the sauce). The sauce should coat, but not swamp, the macaroni. Sprinkle with the oregano and mix together carefully.

5 Transfer the macaroni and meatballs to a large baking dish and top with grated Parmesan. Cook in the oven for 15 minutes.

6 Finish off under a hot grill to bubble and brown the cheese.

meat feast calzone

Rule 1: never trust a restaurant that sells massive pizzas. The heat of the oven cannot possibly cook the middle of the pizza base, so it'll be soggy.
Rule 2: only use the finest ingredients. Cheap salami = disappointing eating.
Rule 3 (this is Tim's rule): all things pickled are brilliant.

Serves 4
For the dough
225g plain strong flour,
   plus extra, for dusting
90ml milk
2 tsp dried yeast
25ml olive oil
pinch of salt

For the filling
150g cherry tomatoes, halved
200g buffalo mozzarella,
   roughly torn
200g assorted Italian meats
(salami, Parma ham, prosciutto
   etc.), cut into strips
1 tbsp capers, rinsed,
   drained, chopped
30g grated Parmesan

top tip:
When you roll dough, always roll, then turn it by 90 degrees, roll, then turn by 90 degrees again. This will ensure that you make a perfect circle. (Also applies to pastry.)

Serve the calzone with a selection of Italian pickles.

The dough
1 Preheat the oven to 230°C/450°F/gas mark 8.

2 Sift the flour into a bowl.

3 In a small saucepan, over a low heat, gently warm the milk.

4 In a bowl mix together 50ml warm water, the warm milk and the yeast. Add to the flour and mix together to form a dough.

5 On a lightly floured surface, knead the dough for 5 minutes.

6 Add the olive oil to the dough and knead to combine. Return the dough to the bowl, cover with cling film and leave somewhere warm for 2 hours, until well risen and springy.

7 Add the salt to the dough, knead again and divide into four equal-sized portions. Roll each portion into a ball.

8 Place each ball on a lightly floured surface and roll out into 20cm circles.

To assemble the calzone
1 Combine the tomatoes, cheese, meats, capers and Parmesan in a bowl.

2 Place one quarter of the mixture onto one half of each circle, leaving a 2cm border. Brush the edges with water and fold the pastry over to cover the filling. Pinch the edges to seal.

3 Place on a baking sheet and cook in the oven for 8 minutes, until the dough is cooked through and the filling is hot.

smoked cheese sausages

Lovejoy was horrified to discover a sausage without meat in it…until he tasted them. These guys have all the flavour of a meaty banger (lots of seasoning) and the fat content in the cheese makes for a good eat.

Makes 8 sausages

300g Lancashire smoked cheese, grated or crumbled
100g fresh breadcrumbs
4 spring onions, chopped
15g fresh thyme, chopped
15g fresh parsley, chopped
2 free-range eggs
1–2 free-range egg yolks
25ml milk
1 garlic clove, crushed
salt and freshly ground black pepper
100ml vegetable oil
350g Maris Piper potatoes
75g butter

Serve the sausages with the sautéed potatoes and a large spoonful of tomato chutney.

1 Place the cheese, breadcrumbs, spring onion, thyme, parsley, all the eggs, the milk and garlic in a large bowl. Season, to taste, with salt and pepper. Using your hands mix everything together well. Check the seasoning and make it a bit more peppery than you would usually have it – the mixture loses a bit of its power as it chills and cooks. Chill the mixture in the fridge for 2 hours.

2 Peel and cube the potatoes and cook in boiling salted water for 10 minutes. Drain and dry on kitchen paper.

3 Remove the mixture from the fridge and mould it into sausage shapes. You should get about 8 decent-sized bangers out of the mix, depending how big you like your sausages…

4 Heat the oil in a frying pan and fry the sausages for about 5 minutes until they are golden. Drain well on some kitchen paper. (You can either deep-fry or shallow-fry the sausages. Deep-frying brings out the best flavours and textures.)

5 Meanwhile, melt the butter in a frying pan and fry the potatoes for 4–5 minutes, until they have coloured and are a little crispy.

top tip:

Work the sausage mixture with your hands until it feels like modelling clay, otherwise the sausages might fall apart.

beetroot rosti with smoked salmon

If I were king I'd make beetroot our national ingredient. You can fry, roast, pickle, grate, mash and slice it. In these tasty rostis they give a lovely sweetness and a sexy colour.

Serves 4

For the beetroot rosti
2 large Maris Piper potatoes (about 400g)
1 medium beetroot, peeled, coarsely grated
1 garlic clove, crushed
salt and freshly ground black pepper
4–5 tbsp vegetable oil
2 slices smoked salmon

For the horseradish dressing
50g fresh horseradish, peeled, grated
100g crème fraîche
juice of ½ lemon
salt and freshly ground black pepper

top tip:
When you cook the potatoes for the rosti, boil them for 7 minutes exactly. This will ensure that they release enough starch to hold them together, but not too much to make them soggy.

Serve the rosti while they are still warm topped with a piece of smoked salmon, a spoonful of the horseradish dressing, some sprigs of dill and a lemon wedge.

The beetroot rosti

1 Leaving the peel on, scrub the potatoes clean in plenty of water. Place in a saucepan and just cover with water. Bring to the boil and cook at a rolling boil for 7 minutes. Leave in the cooling water for 10 minutes, then drain.

2 When the potatoes are cool enough to handle, peel then grate them into a bowl. Try to use long strikes.

3 Add the grated beetroot and garlic, season, to taste, with salt and pepper and mix together well.

4 Divide and mould the mixture into four patties. Chill in the fridge for 1 hour.

5 Heat the oil in a large frying pan over a medium-high heat. Fry the rostis over a medium heat for about 4–6 minutes each side, until golden all over. Remove and drain on kitchen paper.

The horseradish dressing
Mix the horseradish, crème fraîche and lemon juice in a clean bowl. Season, to taste, with salt and pepper.

haddock and sweetcorn chowder

My ideal Sunday is a massive bowl of this chowder with loads of crusty bread, on a cold day, after a walk in the park. The smell of the smoked haddock and the creamy textures are satisfying… good for bonfire parties, too.

Serves 4

50g unsalted butter
1 large onion, sliced
4 rashers smoked bacon, cut into lardons
250ml whole milk
300ml fish stock
1 large baking potato, peeled, cubed
200g canned sweetcorn kernels
450g smoked, undyed haddock, skin removed, cut into four equal-sized pieces
200ml single cream
100g fresh spinach leaves, shredded
salt and freshly ground pepper
2 tbsp chopped fresh parsley

Serve the chowder in bowls with some crusty bread.

1 Melt the butter in a frying pan over a low heat. Add the onion and fry for about 10 minutes, until soft, but not coloured.

2 Add the bacon lardons and cook for 5 minutes.

3 Add the milk, stock and potato cubes. Bring to boil, then reduce the heat and simmer for 10 minutes, or until the potato is cooked.

4 In a food processor, purée half the sweetcorn kernels. Stir the puréed and whole kernels of sweetcorn into the soup.

5 Add the haddock pieces and the cream, cover the pan and simmer gently for about 8–10 minutes, until the fish is completely cooked through.

6 Fold in the spinach leaves, season, to taste, with salt and pepper and sprinkle with the chopped parsley.

top tip:

Add a squeeze of lemon juice at the end if you want to cut through the creamy heaviness of this dish.

spicy**puy** lentil bake

Puy lentils are the king of the lentil family – regal purple when raw, army green when cooked. They have a nutty flavour and because they're tough little guys they keep their shape for longer. The curry flavours and the baked eggs work brilliantly together in this dish.

Serves 4

For the spicy puy lentil bake

1 tbsp olive oil
1 onion, finely chopped
2 garlic cloves, crushed
2 carrots, finely chopped
2 celery stalks, finely chopped
1 red pepper, finely chopped
1 tbsp tomato purée
1 tbsp hot curry powder
300g canned puy lentils, thoroughly rinsed, drained
600ml vegetable stock
4 free-range eggs
handful of chopped fresh coriander
salt and freshly ground black pepper
4 pinches paprika

For the cucumber raita

1 small cucumber, diced
1 tbsp chopped mint
300ml Greek yoghurt
salt and freshly ground black pepper
1 tsp cayenne pepper

To serve, carefully spoon a portion of the lentils with an egg onto each plate. Place a warmed naan bread alongside each plate and serve with a bowl of the cucumber raita.

The spicy puy lentil bake

1 Heat the oil in a large frying pan with a lid over a medium heat. Add the onion, garlic, carrot, celery and red pepper and fry gently for about 10 minutes, until softened and starting to colour.

2 Add the tomato purée and curry powder and cook for 5 minutes.

3 Add the lentils and stock and bring to the boil. Reduce the heat, cover with a lid and simmer for 15–20 minutes, or until the lentils are soft.

4 Make four 'wells' in the lentil mixture and crack an egg into each hole. Cover the pan with a lid for 4 minutes, or until the eggs are cooked to your liking.

5 Sprinkle with coriander and season, to taste, with salt and pepper. Add a pinch of paprika to the top of each egg.

The cucumber raita

Mix the cucumber, mint, yoghurt and cayenne pepper in a bowl. Season, to taste, with salt and pepper, and chill.

top tip:

It's a myth that you need to soak puy lentils. Just be sure to wash them thoroughly.

smoked
mackerel
kedgeree

Fish for brunch may seem like a step too far, but give it a go. I've used risotto rice in this as it holds the curry flavours so well and the smoked fish really cranks up the flavour. My dad loves this one.

Serves 4

1 tbsp olive oil
250g black pudding, sliced into rounds
75g butter
1 onion, finely chopped
250g Arborio or risotto rice
1.25 litres warm chicken stock
4 fresh mackerel fillets
1½ heaped tsp curry powder
250g smoked mackerel fillets
4 free-range eggs, hard boiled, shell removed, chopped
2 tbsp chopped fresh coriander

Serve the kedgeree in bowls garnished with a little freshly grated nutmeg.

1 Place the oil in a frying pan and heat over a medium heat. Fry the black pudding rounds until crisp, then remove and set aside.

2 Melt the butter in the same pan and when it is foaming, fry the onion for about 3 minutes, until soft.

3 Add the rice and stir well to coat the grains in the butter.

4 Add a ladleful of stock, stir well and once it has been absorbed, add another ladleful. Repeat, stirring continuously, until the rice is just cooked but slightly sticky. This may take up to 40 minutes.

5 Meanwhile, when the rice is nearly ready, grill the fresh mackerel fillets for 3–4 minutes each side, until cooked through.

6 When the rice is cooked, add the curry powder and stir to mix.

7 Flake the smoked mackerel fillets (remove any skin and bones) and stir into the rice mixture.

8 Add the eggs, black pudding and coriander. Stir gently to combine. Serve each portion with a grilled mackerel fillet.

top tip:
Make sure the stock you use to cook the rice is warm, otherwise the dish won't come together properly.

smoked cheese and potato cakes

with minted pea purée

This is as simple and delicious as a Hollywood starlet. What could be better than mashed spuds and smoked cheese, deep fried with mushy peas…apart from the aforementioned starlet.

Makes 4 large cakes
For the smoked cheese and potato cakes
4 medium (about 500g) Maris Piper potatoes
1 tbsp olive oil
2 white onions, sliced
1 garlic clove, crushed
salt and freshly ground black pepper
350g smoked Lancashire cheese, grated
75g plain flour
1 large egg, beaten
75g Polenta
400ml vegetable oil

For the minted pea purée
2 tbsp olive oil
4 shallots, chopped
100ml white wine
100ml chicken stock
500g frozen peas
2–3 tbsp chopped mint
2 tbsp crème fraîche

Serve the smoked cheese cakes on the pea purée, garnished with a sprig of fresh mint.

The smoked cheese and potato cakes
1 Peel 3 potatoes and cook in a large pan of boiling salted water until soft. Drain and mash.

2 Grate the remaining potato and squeeze them through a tea towel to release any excess water.

3 Heat the oil in a frying pan over a very low heat and fry the onions for about 10 minutes, until soft.

4 Combine all the potatoes, onions, cheese and garlic in a large bowl. Season with salt and pepper and mix together well.

5 Using your hands, mould the mixture into four cakes.

6 Place the flour in a shallow bowl and the beaten egg in another. Dip each potato cake into the flour to cover. Dip the floured potato cake in the beaten egg, and then in the polenta to coat thoroughly.

7 Pour the vegetable oil in a deep, heavy-bottomed saucepan, ensuring that it is no more than two-thirds full. Heat over a medium flame. When you can drop a breadcrumb into the oil and it sizzles and turns brown, it is hot enough to cook the potato cakes. (It will be about 180°C/350°F, which you can check using a kitchen thermometer. Needless to say, be very careful with the hot oil and never leave it unattended.)

8 Carefully place the potato cakes in the hot oil and deep-fry for about 4 minutes, until they are golden-brown. Remove with a slotted spoon and drain on some kitchen paper.

top tip:

For the pea purée, don't cook the frozen peas first – just thaw them. Otherwise, they might lose their colour. If you want to heat the purée do so after you've blended it.

The minted pea purée

1 Heat the oil in a frying pan over a medium heat and fry the shallots for 2–3 minutes, until soft. Pour in the wine, bring to the boil and reduce the heat to low. Add the stock, bring to boil, remove from the heat and allow to cool a little.

2 In a food processor, blend the mixture with the peas and mint until it forms a purée. Don't over blend. The peas should still retain some shape.

3 Fold in the crème fraîche to achieve a creamy texture.

breakfast frittata

This is a posh omelette, really. If you have the folks staying, this is a great dish to make and serve in the pan, then let everyone dive in and practise their elbowing technique to get some…or is that just my family?

Serves 4

65g unsalted butter
2 onions, sliced
1 garlic clove, chopped
4 pork sausages (Gloucester Old Spot sausages are good), cooked, sliced
6 large free-range eggs
125ml double cream
1 tbsp of thyme
salt and freshly ground black pepper

Serve portions of the frittata with baked beans, a large spoonful of black caviar (or black lumpfish roe), garnished with flat-leaf parsley.

1 Melt the butter in a large frying pan over a low heat and cook the onions and garlic gently for 15–20 minutes, until soft.

2 Add the sliced sausages to the pan and stir to combine.

3 Preheat the grill to its highest setting. Whisk the eggs, cream and thyme together and season well with salt and pepper. Pour over the sausage and onion mix and cook gently over a medium heat for 3–5 minutes, until the eggs are just set.

4 Place under the hot grill for 3–4 minutes, until the frittata puffs up and turns golden brown.

5 Turn out onto a large plate and cut into quarters.

top tip:

When you've added the egg mixture to the pan, agitate the surface, so that it has a good, even surface.

chicken
stroganoff pie

This chicken Stroganoff is great on its own, but with a bit of puff pastry slapped on top, it's destined to be a pub classic in your own kitchen.

Serves 4

300g chicken breasts, cut into strips
2 tbsp smoked paprika
salt and freshly ground black pepper
2 tbsp vegetable oil
50g butter
100g bacon lardons
1 onion, sliced
50g button mushrooms, sliced
50g Portobello or field mushrooms, sliced
1 garlic clove, crushed
50ml brandy
150ml chicken stock
125ml soured cream
4 pieces of ready-rolled puff pastry, each cut 1.5cm wider than the size of four individual ovenproof pie dishes (approx. 11cm deep)
1 free-range egg, beaten

Serve the chicken pies with bowls of pickled red cabbage or pickled beetroot.

1 Preheat the oven to 200°C/400°F/gas mark 6.

2 Dust the chicken strips with half the paprika and season with salt and pepper.

3 Heat the oil in a pan until it is smoking hot. Fry the chicken strips quickly, turning occasionally, until golden-brown all over. Remove from the heat and keep warm.

4 Melt the butter in the same frying pan, and fry the bacon lardons for 2–3 minutes, until golden. Stir in the onion and cook for 4–5 minutes, until soft and slightly golden.

5 Add the sliced mushrooms and garlic and cook for a couple of minutes to soften.

6 Add the brandy and carefully set alight. (Don't worry if it doesn't flame, cooking it will get rid of the alcohol.)

7 Add the stock and bring to the boil. Cook until the liquid has reduced by half.

8 Add the soured cream and remaining tablespoon of paprika. Stir well and simmer until the sauce has reduced to the consistency of thick double cream.

9 Pop the chicken back in the pan to warm through. Check the seasoning.

10 Divide the chicken and cream mixture between the four individual pie dishes.

11 Brush some beaten egg around the top outside edges of the dishes, then press the pastry lids onto the top of the dishes. Brush generously with the beaten egg.

top tip:

To get a crispy pastry topping, place the pies on the bottom shelf of your oven for a few minutes, before moving them up.

12 Cut out a little vent in the top of each pie, for the steam to escape while cooking. Cook in the oven for 20 minutes, or until the pie tops are crisp and golden.

13 Remove the pies from the oven and leave to cool a little before serving.

pork loin with fig and balsamic vinegar

Pork loin has a delicate flavour, so the cumin helps it fight for attention with the fig and balsamic dressing.

Serves 4

For the pork loins
2 x 350g pork loins, each cut in half across the width
pinch of cumin
salt and freshly ground black pepper

For the fig and balsamic dressing
50g butter
75ml balsamic vinegar
75g soft dark brown sugar
zest and juice ½ orange
6–8 figs, quartered
1 pomegranate, seeds only
50g shelled pistachios

Serve slices of the pork with watercress. Spoon the sauce over the top and serve with hot roast potatoes (or fat chips).

The pork loins

1 Preheat the oven to 200°C/400°F/gas mark 6

2 Season the pork with salt and pepper.

3 Melt a little of the butter in a large ovenproof pan over a medium heat. Stir in the cumin and add the pork. Brown the pork on all sides, to seal the meat.

4 Cover the pan with foil and transfer to the oven for about 12 minutes, until cooked through.

The fig and balsamic dressing

1 Heat the sugar and the rest of the butter slowly in a heavy-bottomed saucepan until they begin to caramelise (be careful it doesn't melt too quickly and burn). Add the balsamic vinegar and stir to form a syrup.

2 Remove the pan from the heat and immediately add the figs, pomegranate seeds, orange zest and pistachio nuts, coating them well in the syrup.

top tip:

Pork can be rather bland, so try seasoning it with celery salt or paprika as an alternative to salt and pepper.

classic chicken caesar salad

How many rubbish Caesar salads have you eaten over the past few years? I've eaten a million, at least – so, remember only cos or Little Gem lettuce, you must have anchovies, there are no tomatoes and this dressing rocks.

Serves 4

For the salad
2 chicken breasts, skin and
  knuckle bone attached
salt and freshly ground black
  pepper
1 tbsp vegetable oil
150ml chicken stock
1 cos or Little Gem lettuce, torn
12 anchovies in vinegar

For the croûtons
200g white bread, cut into cubes
pinch of salt
100ml olive oil

For the dressing
75g Parmesan, grated
1 tbsp white wine vinegar
125g mayonnaise
1 tbsp Dijon mustard
2 canned anchovy fillets, rinsed
pinch of salt
1 small garlic clove, crushed
30ml olive oil

top tip:

Try not to touch the salad leaves when you dress them, as they could bruise. Pour the dressing over and swirl around the bowl to coat.

Serve the salad garnished with Parmesan shavings.

The salad

1 Preheat the oven to 200°C/400°F/gas mark 6.

2 Season the chicken with salt and freshly ground black pepper.

3 Heat the oil in a frying pan over a medium heat and cook the chicken, skin-side down, for 5 minutes, until the skin is crisp and golden. (Make sure that the pan isn't too hot.)

4 Flip the breasts over and fry for another 1–2 minutes.

5 Transfer the chicken breasts (skin-side up) to an ovenproof dish and pour the stock around the meat (try not to pour the stock directly over the meat). Cook the chicken in the oven for 20 minutes, until completely cooked through. Allow to cool a little.

The croûtons

Spread the bread cubes out on a baking tray. Sprinkle with salt and drizzle with oil, then pop in the bottom of the oven for about 5 minutes until golden brown and crispy.

The dressing

Blend the Parmesan and vinegar in a food processor until very smooth. Add the mayonnaise, mustard, anchovy fillets, salt, garlic and olive oil and blend again until smooth.

To assemble the Caesar salad

Place the lettuce in a bowl and dress the leaves with some of the dressing. Add the croûtons and transfer the salad to individual bowls. Add three anchovies to each bowl and drizzle over a little more of the dressing. Carve the chicken breasts into thick slices and place half a breast over each salad.

5

dishes
to
impress

tomato and anchovy
tarte tatin

smoked duck
and sesame potatoes

stuffed beef tomatoes

home-made chicken kiev

prawn and broccoli
stir-fry

roasted leeks in ham

smoked mackerel pâté

smoked trout, artichoke
and potato salad

salmon and sea
bass ceviche

king prawn pad thai

asparagus with poached
egg and bacon

pancetta and mozzarella

tomato and anchovy tarte tatin

Apple tarte Tatin is basically an upside down caramelised apple tart, created by accident by the Tatin sisters. The technique can be used with savoury food too, like this tomato tart.

Serves 6

30g unsalted butter

30g caster sugar

4 salted anchovies, rinsed, finely chopped

5 plum tomatoes, cut in half lengthways

salt and freshly ground black pepper

⅔ of a 375g pack ready-rolled puff pastry (to fit over a 20cm-diameter ovenproof frying pan)

1 free-range egg, beaten

Cut the tarte tatin into wedges and serve with a handful of watercress.

1 Preheat the oven to 200°C/400°F/gas mark 6.

2 Melt the butter in a 20cm-diameter ovenproof frying pan until it begins to foam. Add the sugar and cook gently without stirring until it caramelises to a golden colour.

3 Add the anchovies and then place the tomatoes cut-side down in the pan. Season with salt and pepper, cook for 3 minutes, then remove from the heat.

4 Press the pastry over the tomatoes and anchovies while they are still in the pan. Tuck the edges of the pastry into the pan and brush with the beaten egg.

5 Cook in the oven for 25–35 minutes, until golden and crisp.

6 Remove from the oven and leave in the pan for 5 minutes. Carefully turn out of the pan 'upside-down' onto a plate, so that the pastry forms the base. Leave to cool a little.

top tip:

Cooking the anchovies in the pan, until they begin to melt, will prevent them from making the final dish too salty.

smoked duck and sesame potatoes
with plum dressing

I love duck, it's just so scrummy. Teamed with tasty spuds and a delicious plum dressing (that you CANNOT swap for shop-bought hoi sin – PLEASE!)… this will not disappoint.

Serves 4

For the duck and sesame potatoes

2–3 tbsp olive oil
2 baking spuds, peeled, cubed (chuck away the uneven ends)
salt and freshly ground black pepper
50g sesame seeds
splash light soy sauce
mixed salad leaves (mint, Little Gem, chard etc.)
2 smoked duck breasts, sliced

For the plum dressing

100ml plum sauce
50ml rice wine vinegar
1 chilli, finely chopped
juice of 1 lime
1 tbsp chopped fresh coriander

This goes brilliantly with a glass of warm sake.

The duck and sesame potatoes

1 Preheat the oven to 200°C/400°F/gas mark 6.

2 In the oven, heat the oil in an ovenproof dish until it is smoking hot. Chuck in the spuds and season with salt and pepper. Roast for 30 minutes, until they are crisp and golden. (Give 'em a shake every now and then.)

3 Remove the potatoes from the oven and toss in the sesame seeds and soy sauce.

4 Toss the salad leaves in the dressing (see recipe below) and pile onto plates. Scatter with the spuds and arrange the sliced duck over the top.

The plum dressing

Mix together the plum sauce, rice wine vinegar, chilli, lime juice and coriander in a bowl.

top tip:

Make sure the oil is already very hot before you add the potato cubes, rather than pouring cold oil over them. This will help them to crisp up. (Good for roasties, too.)

stuffed beef tomatoes

Since I've known Tim his kitchen skills have got better and better. You need a delicate touch to scoop out the middle of the tomatoes in this recipe, so take your time and be thorough, because, once you've broken the flesh on the tomato, you can't stick it back together – just ask Tim.

Serves 4

4 beef tomatoes, skinned
125g butter
salt and freshly ground black
    pepper
olive oil, to drizzle
100g white breadcrumbs
100g flaked toasted almonds
1 tbsp chopped fresh parsley
1 tsp crushed garlic

Serve each tomato on a handful of fresh herb salad. Drizzle with a little more olive oil and black pepper.

1 Preheat the oven to 180°C/350°F/gas mark 4.

2 Slice the tops off the beef tomatoes. Reserving the juice, scoop out and discard the seeds and core with a spoon.

3 Melt the butter in a small saucepan.

4 Meanwhile, place the tomatoes on a baking tray and season well with salt and pepper. Drizzle with olive oil and cook in the oven for 5 minutes to just warm through.

5 While the tomatoes are warming, in a bowl, combine the tomato juice, breadcrumbs, flaked almonds, parsley, garlic and melted butter.

6 Remove the tomatoes from the oven and stuff them with the mixture. Drizzle with a little more oil and cook for 10 minutes more in the oven, at the same temperature, or until the stuffing is heated through.

top tip:
Be very gentle when you stuff the tomatoes, otherwise you may split the flesh.

home-made
chicken kiev

If your only experience of chicken Kiev is out of the freezer cabinet then you've probably turned the page already – but hold on there partner. Make these today and feel like a Russian millionaire.

Serves 4

3 garlic cloves, crushed
juice of ½ lemon
salt and freshly ground black pepper
1 tbsp finely chopped tarragon
150g unsalted butter, slightly softened
4 x 175g skinless chicken breasts
2 tbsp plain flour
1 free-range egg, beaten
4 tbsp breadcrumbs
3 tbsp vegetable oil
250g mix of white and wild rice
100g bacon lardons
1 tbsp parsley, chopped
100g toasted pine nuts

Keep with the retro theme and serve the Kievs with a glass of Black Tower or Blue Nun wine.

1 In a bowl, beat the garlic, lemon juice, salt and pepper, tarragon and softened butter together, until well blended. Divide into four, wrap in foil, shape into flattish cylinders and freeze for 5 minutes.

2 Using a sharp knife cut a pocket into the side of each of the chicken breasts.

3 Stuff the frozen butter into the pockets of each chicken breast and pull the flesh back over to cover.

4 Cover the chicken breasts in the flour, dip into the beaten egg then coat thoroughly in the breadcrumbs.

5 Preheat the oven to 200°C/400°F/gas mark 6.

6 Heat 2 tbsp oil in a frying pan over a medium heat. Fry the chicken on all sides in the pan, until lightly browned.

7 Transfer the chicken to a baking tray and cook in the oven for 18–20 minutes, until golden brown and cooked through.

8 Meanwhile, cook the rice in a large pan of lightly salted water according to the packet instructions. Drain.

9 Heat the remaining oil in a frying pan over a medium heat and cook the bacon lardons for 5–10 minutes, until browned.

10 In a bowl, combine the cooked rice with the bacon, parsley, pine nuts and butter. Pack the rice mixture into a serving cup, place the chicken alongside and watch the butter ooze out as you slice into it.

top tip:

Although the butter needs to be softened before you pack it inside the chicken, make sure it isn't melted. Otherwise, it will leak out as the chicken cooks.

prawn
and purple sprouting
broccoli
stir-fry

Over used, badly done and with too many ingredients, that's the problem with a stir-fry. The genius that is Ken Hom made us all buy a wok, so in honour of King Ken, keep it simple, tasty and keep the ingredients moving.

Serves 4
300g purple sprouting broccoli
2 tbsp vegetable oil
16 king prawns, raw, shelled
1½ tsp dried chilli flakes
1 garlic clove, sliced
juice of 1 lemon
1 head pak choi, finely sliced
2 canned anchovies, drained
 rinsed, finely chopped
salt and freshly ground black
 pepper

Serve the stir-fry in bowls, sprinkled with sesame seeds and a little grated nutmeg.

1 Heat a large saucepan of boiling water. Fill a large bowl with ice-cold water. When the hot water has reached a rolling boil add the broccoli. Cook for 1–2 minutes, until just tender, then remove and refresh in the cold water. This will retain the broccoli's texture and colour.

2 Heat 1 tbsp oil in a wok or deep frying pan and when very hot add the prawns and fry for 2–3 minutes, tossing and stirring them until pink.

3 Remove the prawns from the pan and set aside. Heat the remaining oil in the wok and when hot add the broccoli, chilli flakes and garlic. Stir-fry over a high heat for a further 2 minutes.

4 Add the lemon juice, pak choi, anchovies and prawns and season with salt and pepper. Cook for 1–2 minutes, until completely heated through.

top tip:
A good way to chop herbs or other leaves is to roll them up into a ball and chop that, so you get nice neat strips.

roasted leeks in ham
with lemon vinaigrette

This is the very first dish we made on the show and still a fave of mine. It is very easy to make and pretty difficult to get wrong.

Serves 4

For the leeks in ham
6 leeks, washed thoroughly
salt and freshly ground black
    pepper
50ml olive oil
12 slices of Cumbrian
    air-dried ham

For the lemon vinaigrette
½ tbsp Dijon mustard
25ml white wine vinegar
½ tbsp thyme leaves, picked
½ garlic clove, crushed
juice of ½ small lemon
100ml extra virgin olive oil
salt and freshly ground black
    pepper

top tip:
To pick thyme, just run your fingers down the stalk and all the leaves will fall off, rather than picking each individual one off.

Serve the ham-wrapped leeks garnished with thyme, a little pepper and, perhaps, a few Parmesan shavings.

The leeks in ham

1 Preheat the oven to 200°C/400°F/gas mark 6.

2 Trim the leeks and cut each one in half, on the diagonal, so you have 12 even-sized pieces.

3 Season with salt and pepper and place in an oven-proof dish. Drizzle with the olive oil and roast in the oven for 25 minutes, until they are soft.

4 Once the leeks are cooked, remove from the oven and peel off the crispy outer layer.

5 Wrap a piece of ham around each piece of leek. The flavours of the ham will absorb into the leek.

6 Place three leek pieces onto each plate and spoon over some of the dressing (see recipe below).

The lemon vinaigrette
Whisk the mustard and vinegar together. Add the thyme, garlic and lemon juice, then slowly add the olive oil, whisking continuously. Season, to taste, with salt and pepper.

smoked mackerel pâté
with caramelised shallots

My favourite type of dishes are ones like this – it tastes amazing, it looks difficult and yet it's a doddle to make. The end result: happy dining companions and brownie points all round.

Serves 4-6

2 peppered smoked mackerel fillets, skinned, flaked
150g full-fat cream cheese
75g ricotta
juice of ½ lemon
salt and freshly ground black pepper
50g unsalted butter
75g Demerara sugar
8 banana shallots, peeled (keep whole)
30ml balsamic vinegar
slices of brioche, to serve

Serve the pâté with a couple of slices of Parma ham for an even more decadent combination of flavours.

1 Preheat the oven to 200°C/400°F/gas mark 6.

2 Melt the butter in an ovenproof dish on the hob. Add the sugar and cook until it begins to melt.

3 Add the shallots, toss in the sugary mixture and roast in the oven for 30 minutes, until tender. Shake occasionally.

4 Blend the mackerel, cream cheese, ricotta and lemon juice in a food processor until smooth. Season, to taste, with a little salt and pepper.

5 Divide the pâté between small ramekins and chill in the fridge.

6 As soon as the shallots are cooked, remove from the oven, add the vinegar and mix well.

7 Toast the slices of brioche.

8 Serve a ramekin of pâté each, with the toasted brioche and the shallots to the side.

top tip:

Ovens vary a lot, so if you find after cooking the shallots, that they aren't quite soft enough, don't be afraid to leave them in for longer, to soften and caramelise more – they will only get better.

smoked trout, artichoke and potato salad

When you read through the ingredients on this, you might think they don't go together – cottage cheese and smoked trout? But they really do, the sum of all parts never fails to leave even the most sceptical of people (calling Mr Lovejoy) wanting more.

Serves 4

For the trout, artichoke and potato salad
8-12 Jersey Royal new potatoes
½ red onion, very finely sliced into half-moons
4 griddled artichokes in olive oil, drained
4 smoked trout fillets, flaked
1 tbsp chopped dill
4 tbsp cottage cheese

For the dressing
30ml lemon juice
200ml extra virgin olive oil
30ml sherry vinegar
salt and freshly ground black pepper

Serve the salad garnished with extra dill.

The trout, artichoke and potato salad

1 Cook the potatoes in a large saucepan of boiling salted water for 15–20 minutes, until they are tender. Drain and set aside.

2 In a bowl, toss the spuds in the dressing (see recipe below) and mix together with the onion, artichoke, trout and dill. Stir well, to coat everything in the dressing. Serve each portion topped with a spoonful of cottage cheese.

The dressing

Whisk together the lemon juice, olive oil and sherry vinegar. Season with salt and pepper.

top tip:

Don't ever peel Jersey Royal potatoes as all the flavour is in the skin.

salmon and sea bass ceviche

Raw fish – not for me…oh, yes it is. This is simply the best way to use really fresh fish. It brings out so much flavour and is so refreshing. Another Lovejoy Top Ten smash.

Serves 4

For the salmon and sea bass ceviche
250g very fresh sea bass fillets, cut into 2.5cm pieces
250g very fresh salmon fillets cut into 2.5cm pieces
1 grapefruit
juice of ½ orange
juice of 2 limes,
2 bird's eye chillies, chopped
3 spring onions, very finely chopped
1 garlic clove, crushed
salt and freshly ground black pepper
1 tbsp chopped mint leaves

For the French toast
6 thick slices bread, preferably a day old
4 free-range eggs
200ml milk
pinch salt
50–75g butter

Serve the salad garnished with a few grapefruit segments and the French toast.

The salmon and sea bass ceviche

1 Place the fish in a bowl and sprinkle with the juice of half the grapefruit, the orange juice and the lime juice. Separate out the segments of the remaining grapefruit half and set aside to use as a garnish.

2 Add the chilli, spring onions and garlic and season with a little salt and pepper.

3 Cover the bowl and chill in the fridge for at least 40 minutes, but up to 4 hours for a fuller flavour.

4 Just before serving add the mint to the bowl and mix to combine.

The French toast

1 In a shallow bowl, beat the eggs, milk and salt together.

2 Heat a knob of the butter in a frying pan over a medium heat until it starts to foam.

3 Dunk each slice of bread in the egg mixture for a few seconds, turning until well coated.

4 Cook the slices, two at a time, in the pan, turning once, until golden and crisp. Repeat with the remaining bread and butter. Serve while hot.

top tip:
Make sure that you use really, really fresh fish for this.

king prawn pad thai

I think I could live on this. I adore Thai food and I reckon you can gauge a Thai restaurant by the quality of this dish. So make mine and then go and taste-test.

Serves 4
250g fine rice noodles
50ml vegetable oil
1 garlic clove, sliced
20 king prawns, shelled
2 free-range eggs, beaten
1 tbsp shrimp paste
75g roasted peanuts
½ tsp chilli flakes
225g bean sprouts
1–2 tsp sugar
2 tbsp soy sauce
2 tbsp fish sauce

Serve the pad Thai in bowls, garnished with chopped coriander and a squeeze of lime.

1 Soak the noodles in a bowl of warm water for 20 minutes, to soften. Drain.

2 Heat the oil in a wok over a high heat. Add the garlic and prawns and stir-fry for 2 minutes. Remove and set aside.

3 Add the eggs to the wok and spread out as though you were cooking an omelette. Once it has cooked, break up the egg into chunks and set aside with the garlic and prawns.

4 Stir-fry the shrimp paste, peanuts and chilli for a minute.

5 Add the noodles, bean sprouts, sugar, soy sauce and fish sauce and stir-fry to warm through. Fold in the eggs and prawns and stir gently to combine.

top tip:

Always check the packet before using noodles as their preparation instructions will differ. But, usually, you will only need to soak them in hot water, not boil them as you would pasta.

asparagus with poached egg and bacon

This looks difficult, but with a bit of care is very straightforward. Particularly good in the British asparagus season.

Serves 4

large bunch English asparagus
12 rashers dry cured English
   streaky bacon
4 free-range eggs

For the Hollandaise sauce

250g butter
juice 1 lemon
sprig fresh tarragon
10ml white wine vinegar
2 free-range egg yolks

Serve with thickly sliced toasted bread soldiers to dip into the runny egg. Heaven.

1 Heat the grill to its highest setting.

2 Trim off the tough ends from the asparagus and cook in boiling water for one minute. Remove and drain on kitchen paper.

3 Heat a griddle pan until very hot. Cook the asparagus on the griddle, turning occasionally, for 1–2 minutes, until charred.

4 Grill the bacon for about 4 minutes, turning once, until crisp.

5 Half fill a frying pan with water and bring to the boil. Reduce the heat and gently break in an egg. Cook for one minute, remove from the heat and leave covered until the white is firm. Carefully remove the cooked egg with a slotted spoon, set aside and cover to keep warm while you poach the three remaining eggs.

6 Place three asparagus spears on a plate, season with salt and pepper. Sit a poached egg on top and three rashers of bacon alongside. Place a spoonful of dressing (see recipe below) on top of each egg.

The Hollandaise sauce

1 Melt the butter in a pan slowly over a low heat. When it has melted, skim off the cloudy surface (the impurities), leaving behind the clearer, clarified, butter.

2 Place the lemon juice, tarragon and vinegar in a small pan. Warm gently over a low heat. Remove the tarragon sprig.

3 Place the egg yolks in a bowl and whisk lightly. Add the lemon juice and vinegar mixture and continue whisking.

4 Slowly add the clarified butter, whisking to emulsify and create a mayonnaise-like consistency. Season with salt and pepper.

top tip:

If the Hollandaise sauce begins to split, add a drop of warm water to bring it back together.

dishes to impress

pancetta and mozzarella
with fig jam

This is really just fancy cheese on toast. It looks amazing, tastes even better and should definitely become one of your signature dishes.

Serves 4

For the pancetta and mozzarella

400g buffalo mozzarella (top quality)
4 tbsp chopped fresh thyme
freshly ground black pepper
8 slices pancetta
2 tbsp vegetable oil

For the fig jam

2 tbsp vegetable oil
1 onion, finely sliced
200g figs, quartered
100g runny honey
75ml red wine vinegar
1 tbsp orange blossom water, optional

Serve the cheese parcels on a thick slice of toasted walnut bread with a dollop of the fig jam on top.

The pancetta and mozzarella

1 Cut the cheese into eight equal-sized pieces. Roll in the thyme and sprinkle with freshly ground black pepper.

2 Roll each piece of cheese in a piece of the pancetta and secure with a cocktail stick.

3 Heat the oil in a frying pan over a medium-high heat and fry the mozzarella parcels on all sides for about 4–7 minutes, until the pancetta is cooked.

The fig jam

1 Heat the oil in a frying pan over a medium heat and fry the onion for 4–5 minutes, until soft.

2 Add the figs, honey and vinegar and bring slowly to the boil. Reduce the heat and simmer for 10–20 minutes, until thick, then add the orange blossom water, if using.

top tip:

To prevent the mozzarella becoming soggy when it is fried, pat it dry with kitchen paper before you use it.

index

A

Almond rolled goat's cheese 74–75

American pancakes with bacon 40

anchovies

Mozzarella skewers with tomato and anchovy sauce 76

Tomato and anchovy tarte tatin 117

Asparagus with poached egg and bacon 137

avocados

Guacamole 27

Tartare of salmon and avocado with prawns and pink grapefruit 46

B

bacon

American pancakes with bacon 40

Asparagus with poached egg and bacon 137

Bacon, bran and cinnamon muffins 39

Basil and lime mayonnaise 34

bass, sea

Salmon and sea bass ceviche 132

beans, white

Posh beans on toast 52

beef

Baked macaroni and meatballs 90–91

Beef empanadas 20

beetroot

Beetroot rosti with smoked salmon 96

Roast beetroot 74

bhajis

Seafood bhajis with yoghurt dressing 79

Breakfast burritos 70

Breakfast frittata 107

C

calzone

Meat feast calzone 93

ceviche

Salmon and sea bass ceviche 132

cheese

Almond rolled goat's cheese 74–75

Cheese and potato pasty with walnut pastry 24–25

Cheesy potato pies 29

Mushroom and caramelised onion rarebit 49

Smoked cheese and potato cakes with minted pea purée 104–105

Smoked cheese sausages 95

see also mozzarella

chicken

Chicken Kiev 123

Chicken koftas with yoghurt dressing 66

Chicken Stroganoff pie 108–109

Classic chicken Caesar salad 112

Coronation chicken salad 59

Crispy fried chicken with guacamole 27

Poached chicken salad with red pepper dressing 42

chowder

Haddock and sweetcorn chowder 99

Chutney 25

Classic chicken Caesar salad 112

Corned beef fritters 18

Coronation chicken salad 59

Crab noodle salad with nuoc cham 55

Crispy fried chicken with guacamole 27

Croûtons 112

cucumber

Cucumber raita 100

Yoghurt dressing 66

D

Dim sum, Prawn 85

dressings

Fig and balsamic vinegar dressing 111

Horseradish dressing 96

Lemon-chilli dressing 56

Lemon vinaigrettes 50, 127, 131

Plum dressing 118

Red pepper dressing 42

Thousand Island dressing 46

Yoghurt dressings 66, 79

see also sauces

duck, smoked
   Smoked duck and sesame
      potatoes with plum dressing
      118

E
eggs
   Asparagus with poached egg
      and bacon 137
   Breakfast burritos 70
   Breakfast frittata 107
   Huevos rancheros
      (Ranch eggs with kale) 72
   Scotch eggs 13
Empanadas, Beef 20

F
figs
   Fig and balsamic dressing 111
   Fig jam 138
fish
   Beetroot rosti with smoked
      salmon 96
   Haddock and sweetcorn
      chowder 99
   New York smoked salmon
      hash 50
   Poached salmon with peas
      and chorizo 60
   Pollack goujons with tamarind
      sauce 86
   Salmon and sea bass ceviche
      132
   Salmon burgers with basil
      and lime mayonnaise 34
   Salmon sushi rolls 65

Smoked haddock tempura with
   salsa verde 33
Smoked mackerel kedgeree
   103
Smoked mackerel pâté with
   caramelised shallots 128
Smoked trout, artichoke and
   potato salad 131
Tartare of salmon and avocado
   46
Tuna and ricotta fritters with
   tartare sauce 81
Flatbread and spicy houmous 69
French toast 132
Frittata, Breakfast 107
fritters
   Corned beef fritters 18
   Tuna and ricotta fritters with
      tartare sauce 81

G
Guacamole 27

H
haddock, smoked
   Haddock and sweetcorn
      chowder 99
   Smoked haddock tempura with
      salsa verde 33
ham
   Roasted leeks in ham with
      lemon vinaigrette 127
Hollandaise sauce 137
Horseradish dressing 96
Houmous 69
Huevos rancheros 72

K
kedgeree
   Smoked mackerel kedgeree
      103
King prawn pad Thai 134

L
leeks
   Roasted leeks in ham with
      lemon vinaigrette 127
Lemon-chilli dressing 56
Lemon vinaigrettes 50, 127,
   131
lentils
   Spicy puy lentil bake 100

M
Macaroni and meatballs, Baked
   90–91
mackerel, smoked
   Smoked mackerel kedgeree
      103
   Smoked mackerel pâté with
      caramelised shallots 128
mayonnaise
   Basil and lime mayonnaise 34
Meat feast calzone 93
meatballs
   Baked macaroni and meatballs
      90–91
mozzarella
   Mozzarella skewers with
      tomato and anchovy sauce
      76
   Pancetta and mozzarella with
      fig jam 138

Roasted tomatoes and mozzarella with lemon-chilli dressing 56
muffins
  Bacon, bran and cinnamon muffins 39
Mushroom and caramelised onion rarebit 49

N
New York smoked salmon hash 50
noodles
  Crab noodle salad with nuoc cham 55
  Pots of noodles 17
Nuoc cham 55

O
Onion marmalade 18

P
pancakes
  American pancakes with bacon 40
Pancetta and mozzarella with fig jam 138
pasta
  Baked macaroni and meatballs 90–91
  Pasta primavera 45
pastry 20, 24, 82
pasty
  Cheese and potato pasty with walnut pastry 24–25

pâté
  Smoked mackerel pâté with caramelised shallots 128
Pea purée 104, 105
peppers
  Breakfast burritos 70
  Red pepper dressing 42
Pico de gallo 27
pies
  Cheesy potato pies 29
  Chicken Stroganoff pie 108–109
  Pork pie 82
Plum dressing 118
Pollack goujons with tamarind sauce 86
pork
  Pork loin with fig and balsamic vinegar 111
  Pork pies 82
Posh beans on toast 52
potatoes
  Beetroot rosti with smoked salmon 96
  Cheese and potato pasty with walnut pastry 24–25
  Cheesy potato pies 29
  Smoked cheese and potato cakes with minted pea purée 104–105
Pots of noodles 17
prawns
  King prawn pad Thai 134
  Prawn and purple sprouting broccoli stir-fry 124
  Prawn dim sum 85
  Shrimp po'boys 23

R
Raita 100

S
salads
  Classic chicken Caesar salad 112
  Coronation chicken salad 59
  Poached chicken salad with red pepper dressing 42
  Roasted tomatoes and mozzarella with lemon-chilli dressing 56
  Smoked trout, artichoke and potato salad 131
salmon
  Poached salmon with peas and chorizo 60
  Salmon and sea bass ceviche 132
  Salmon burgers with basil and lime mayonnaise 34
  Salmon sushi rolls 65
  Tartare of salmon and avocado with prawns and pink grapefruit 46
salmon, smoked
  Beetroot rosti with smoked salmon 96
  New York smoked salmon hash 50
Salsa verde 33
sauces
  Hollandaise sauce 137
  Salsa verde 33
  Tamarind sauce 86
  Tartare sauce 81

Tomato and anchovy sauce 76
  see also dressings
sausage meat
  Big sausage rolls 14
  Scotch eggs 13
sausages
  Breakfast frittata 107
Scotch eggs 13
seafood see also crab; fish;
  prawns
Seafood bhajis with yoghurt
  dressing 79
shellfish see crab; prawns
Shrimp po'boys 23
smoked mackerel see mackerel,
  smoked
smoked salmon see salmon,
  smoked
smoked trout see trout, smoked
Spicy puy lentil bake 100
squid
  Prawn dim sum 85
stir-fry
  Prawn and purple sprouting
    broccoli stir-fry 124
Stuffed beef tomatoes 121
sushi
  Salmon sushi rolls 65

T
tacos
  Veggie chilli tacos 30
Tamarind sauce 86
Tartare of salmon and avocado
  with prawns and pink
    grapefruit 46
Tartare sauce 81

tempura
  Smoked haddock tempura with
    salsa verde 33
Thousand Island dressing 46
tomatoes
  Mozzarella skewers with
    tomato and anchovy sauce
      76
  Roasted tomatoes and
    mozzarella with lemon-chilli
      dressing 56
  Stuffed beef tomatoes 121
  Tomato and anchovy tarte tatin
    117
tortillas
  Breakfast burritos 70
trout, smoked
  Smoked trout, artichoke and
    potato salad 131
Tuna and ricotta fritters with
  tartare sauce 81

V
Veggie chilli tacos 30
Vinaigrettes, Lemon 50, 127,
  131

Y
Yoghurt dressings 66, 79

acknowledgements

Simon would like to give big love and thanks to everyone connected with *Something for the Weekend* but especially JoJo, Catherine, Henrietta, Claire, Yaz, Dave, Seb, Charlie, both Nicks, Paul, Johnny Mac, Jo, Carla Maria and Jay for making it all possible.

Tim would like to thank Simon for all the food he gets to eat on the show and Amanda Hamilton for being his new on-screen wife.